To Judi, Thank you for the support. May continue to bless. and keep speaking boldness.

Love, Brother Keith

The Prepper and The Preacher: A Spiritual Survival Guide

By Keith Iton
Copyright 2015

Editor: Vicki Barnard
Artwork: Alicia Landry

Dedication Page

This book is dedicated to the memory of three of the most influential men to walk in my life. Words will never express what you all meant to me.

My Uncle Roy
For teaching me to write with a passion and to never fall for propaganda

Pastor John Perault
For teaching me to forgive others and showing me what it means to walk like Christ

My brother Wayne
For boldly leading me to Christ and warning me to always be prepared

Table of Contents

1*Bomb Shelter or Being Under the Shelter of the most High? p.4

2*Food, Farms or Faith? P.12

3*The Hypocrite or The Hypochondriac? P.28

4*Cash for Gold or the Cash Cajole? P.36

5*Smoke the Rock or Speak to the Rock? P.48

6*When there is no doctor? P.57

7*Physical Fitness or Spiritual Fitness? P.68

8*Animal Authority or Authority over the Animals? P.81

9*The Ultimate Bugout Vehicle? P.96

10*AR 15 or An Angel? P.106

11*Disarmament? P.120

12*Racism or Reality? P.128

13*Demons or Depression or Destination? P.136

14*Multiple Confirmations? P.149

15*Change the Weather Or Weather the Change? P.159

16*Gift of Gab? P.172

17*Blind Justice or Justice for the Blind? P.185

18*Your Voice or God's Voice? P.196

Bonus Section

CHAPTER 1

Bomb Shelter VS Being under the Shelter of the Most High

I get asked this question all the time: "Brother Keith, don't you think those people on television with bomb shelters are ridiculous?" My answer is pretty much the same as I am writing this book today. "If they can afford it, why not? But I hope they have a relationship with God".

You see, there are reasons why people around the world build underground shelters or bunkers. It is actually quite normal for people to have underground shelters in the tornado prone parts of the Midwestern United States. These underground bunkers are sometimes referred to as storm shelters. They are reinforced with steel and concrete to keep people safe while the destructive power of the tornado wreaks havoc overhead. Some people have them in certain parts of the eastern United States (Florida, North Carolina, etc.) to defend against hurricanes but they have to make sure they are water tight due to flooding issues. I would like to interject that a storm shelter and a bomb shelter can be one in the same if the situation should arise. However, a bomb shelter provides more than just reinforced walls, it may also have air filtration systems, running water, sleeping quarters, etc.

Some people have the knowledge that the United States has narrowly avoided nuclear war on numerous occasions. We the people were only informed of the Cuban Missile Crisis during the presidency of John F. Kennedy, when in reality our team has fumbled the football on numerous occasions. (Yes, we almost had WWW3!!!) I believe it's only by the grace of God and His divine intervention that we averted the tragedy. Let's face it, human beings are known to make mistakes. People accidently shoot people with guns all the time. In war, a bomber plane can accidently destroy the wrong target. Are humans that much safer with nuclear bombs, especially when greed and evil continue to play a role in international affairs?

Back to my point, some people are justified for their concerns of owning a bomb/storm shelter. I will not ridicule them because I do see the wisdom in certain cases. But I observe a spirit of fear in most other cases. When fear comes upon some people, folly (stupidity) will surely follow.

Let me give you an example of what I mean. There was recent case of a man that lost his temper (maybe his sanity), and decided to threaten to kill his family. The police were called and the family quickly took sanctuary at the neighbor's house. Once the police discovered the family was safe at the next door neighbor's house, they went back to the house in question to arrest the estranged husband. He decided to lock himself in his bomb shelter and threaten the police. The police simply put smoke bombs and tear gas down the ventilation pipe, thus forcing the man to exit the shelter and face arrest. I continue to thank God everyday because the police showed excellent restraint by not shooting the husband dead. The man behaved like a fool on way too many levels for me to write about and he is currently under psychiatric evaluation. Aside from being mentally unstable, the man showed the most common Achilles heel for people who decide to build bomb shelters. Aside from not having the peace of God in his life, which would of kept him from being so foolish, he never protected his supply of air.

You would actually be surprised at the amount of people that do this. They spend thousands of dollars on constructing a bomb shelter and supplying it with emergency supplies, only to have a tiny pipe to supply oxygen to it. They basically build themselves expensive coffins to choke themselves to death. Word to the wise, if you claim you have a bomb shelter, make sure the supply of oxygen is protected. Any desperate marauder with half an IQ will simply try to cut off the air to spoil your goods.

As far as I am concerned, any bomb shelter on earth can be breached by natural or supernatural forces. That is why I do not stress owning one. I recently saw a movie about people living in a massive bomb shelter in a post apocalyptic world. The people were trying there best to get by with day to activities for a few years until someone caught the flu. Needless to say many people had to die from a virus they could not see with the naked eye.

I can hear one or two of you saying, "That does not apply to me because my bomb shelter is small. My immediate family will be with me and no one else."

My reply will be, "Okay then smarty pants, since you have the cure to the flu, may I have a few vials of it for my bug out bag." I have learned to not even argue with people that are unrealistic. My young son caught the flu a few years ago and even though my wife and I were extremely cautious about washing hands, taking extra vitamins, and keeping the place well ventilated, we still caught this nasty bug. I am convinced it was prayer that healed us, because nothing else worked. Other people that caught this strain of the flu virus that year were less fortunate in recovering.

Guess what? There is hope beyond the bomb shelter. During World War 2 a particular city in Europe was being bombed mercilessly bombed the Germans. Massive buildings were being turned to pebbles and dust before the eyes of many. Some people took immediate shelter in church rather than being trampled to death as people ran for their lives in a panic. The fairly large cathedral was connected to all the other buildings on the city block, so it was certain to be destroyed by the bombs or the raging fires that ensued. As the explosions got closer, people began to pray fervently in the church pews. The reverend then instructed the people to sing songs from the hymn book while the organist played the melody. The people sang their hearts out while explosions ripped through there city. Little kids cowered under their parents in fear, while others remained on their knees in deep prayer. After a while they noticed the explosions stopped and the alarm siren became silent. The people walked outside and were amazed at the sight before them. The entire city lay in ruins and every building surrounding the church was destroyed. There was not one broken glass or brick on the church. The entire structure remained untouched during the bombing.

The book of Psalms chapter 91 verse 1 says, "He that dwelleth in the secret place of the most High shall abide under the shadow of the Almighty." The people that day in Europe understood the importance of dwelling in God's presence during their time of need. The people in the church were either in deep prayer or singing songs of praise to God. They also knew they can trust in God because verse 4 of Psalm 91 says "He shall cover thee with his feathers". Have you ever seen a bird cover her young in a violent rain storm? As the heavy rains beat down on the bird and the nest, the young chicks remain untouched and completely dry. Notice how the people in the church remained untouched and dry from the spilling of blood?

There is a hypocrisy among some bomb shelter type preppers that claim to be Christian that does need to be called out. Although I stand firmly against socialism, I will stand for the teachings of Jesus Christ. In the gospels Christ has taught his followers to bless the poor numerous times. Let's just say you have the money for a massive underground bunker that can be self sustaining for weeks because of the preps you fortified it with. God has blessed your business ventures 100 fold enabling you to make preparations for your immediate family. Your next door neighbor however is in a different boat financially. Although he is a devout Christian, his finances are a mess because he was laid off from his job and his wife has cancer. They have 3 young children the same age as your children and they attend the same school. You both have been prepping for quite some time, but he can only afford to put back some extra food for the kids. He had to sell all of his guns and gold to pay the mortgage and the medical bills. If the Russian military begins to bomb your neighborhood, should you let him and his family in the bomb shelter? You may be surprised at some of the answers I have heard from preppers that claim to be Christian.

Shelter from the unseen enemies

I often hear of some preppers speaking of the HAARP project in Alaska. HAARP stands for High Frequency Active Auroral Research Program. According to the United States Military, Its purpose is to analyze the ionosphere for data and communications capabilities. However, military whistle blowers and conspiracy theorists argue that the uses of HAARP are much more nefarious. The rumored uses of HAARP signals range from mind control, weather manipulation, and earthquakes. I won't be ignorant to say it isn't possible because every military in the modern world has some kind of classified technology. Yet, some preppers get fearful of this stuff. A common fear among preppers is if today's equivalent of a Joseph Stalin or Adolph Hitler, wields that kind of weapon, he will use it on the people to consolidate power. I gladly let them know that God is the one that determines your time of death; not a machine and surely not man. If God has determined that you are going to live for 90 years, there is no human being that can stop that plan. Especially if you are under His divine protection.

Thou art my hiding place; thou shalt preserve me from trouble; thou shalt compass me about with songs of deliverance. Selah. (Psalm 32:7)

Let me prove my point: Back on November 13th, 2007, the popular radio show Coast to Coast Am interviewed a former British Intelligence officer named James Casbolt. The interview was quite riveting especially when he discussed the different methods of assassinations. He claimed that the NSA had satellites that were capable of sending aimed signals to a human being to enable heart attacks. However, James Casbolt said that when they try to use the satellite weaponry against someone that is highly spiritual, it was like them throwing a pebble at a tank. No matter how much they turned the satellite signals up, the person could not be assassinated!

Shelter from Spiritual Enemies

Some of you preppers may be living next to a witch. I am not talking about the characters from the Saturday morning cartoons we used to watch as kids, but I mean people that practice occult arts, hypnotism and black magic. If you are prepper that is not protected by the blood of Jesus Christ, a highly tuned witch will have you giving away your preps to satisfy their needs and or even worse, they could try to kill you by conjuring up a demon.

One evening I downloaded an internet broadcast called Omega Man Radio by a gentleman named Shannon Davis. His featured guest that evening was a former high ranking Satanist named Doc Marquis. The guest gave his testimony on how he was born into that particular lifestyle and how he later converted to following Jesus Christ. He confirmed the suspicions of preppers worldwide by saying that their were high ranking Satanists scattered throughout the halls of government worldwide. Yet, the biggest revelation came when he discussed the Satan worshippers attempt to kill a high ranking U.S. general. The plan to them was quite simple: They would conjure up a demon from the unseen realm to kill the general and then when the murder was complete, they send the demon back through the portal to the other dimension. Doc Marquis explained how he and the other Satanists gathered together to do the ancient ritual required to conjure up the demon and they watched it appear and fly straight to the general's home. However, just as fast the demon left, it returned just as quickly. The demon was furious because he was sent to the home of a real Christian. The demon was angry because he was powerless to touch the general and embarrassed. Since the demon was not given any blood, he decided to kill one of the Satanist in the room as punishment. Doc Marquis said that was a pivotal moment in him realizing that Jesus Christ had the most power!

Thou believest that there is one God; thou doest well: the devils also believe, and tremble.
(James 2:19)

I have witnessed and heard numerous cases of witchcraft being used on an unsuspecting person and the results were disastrous. I personally knew of a prepper that used hypnosis on suspecting preppers to bilk them for personal information to use for his advantage at a later time. If you are a prepper and you suspect you are living next to a witch, you should do the following:

1) Ask Jesus into your life and repent of your sins
2) In prayer, plead the blood of Jesus over your family and property.
3) Pray for God to deliver that person to righteousness
4) Ask God to remove the person if they refuse to accept Jesus

That last one is a major deal breaker. When ever I encounter someone that comes around our fellowship, and God lets me know that they have no intention of changing their wicked ways, I simply ask God to remove that person. They are usually gone within a few weeks. In most cases that person is a witch or heavily interacting with demons by way of hardcore drugs or pornography. The reality is there are some people that are quite happy doing what their doing and getting to know Jesus is the farthest thing on their spiritual radar. You do not want such a person in your church, in your home or near your prepping endeavors!

Hopefully, this chapter will enlighten the average prepper to be prepared for all the unseen enemies. An armed looter showing up to your house in the middle of the night is only one facet of being prepared for unwanted visitors. There are unwanted visitors that will try to show up by sneakier means. The bomb shelter will not stop these type of foes, but by being under the shelter of the most high, your protection will be impregnable.

Be sober, be vigilant; because your adversary the devil, as a roaring lion, walketh about, seeking whom he may devour: (1 Peter 5:8)

Chapter 2

Farms, Food, Or Faith?

For those of you out there that do not know me personally, I have long been an advocate of storing extra food for emergencies. Besides being a pastor, I work in the emergency preparedness business. My company sells emergency food products via the internet, gun shows, and preparedness seminars. I understand the "prepper" community better than others because by some accounts I have been called one. I happen to prefer the term "watchman" instead. I watch current events both politically and spiritually to draw my conclusions. Hence the reason I will warn every reader of this book to have a source of not only physical food, but also spiritual food.

My parents actually instilled this belief in me because of their up bringing in the Caribbean islands. They witnessed the massive destruction hurricanes can bring to a community and the lack of food resources during the aftermath. I became aware of this threat when I lived in South Florida for a good portion of my life. Every time a major hurricane would hit South Florida, there would always be some people in panic because they never bothered to prepare for the storm. (Listen up America, Canada, and England.) These would be the people you would later see on television getting into altercations with people over food and water. In many cases the situation could have been avoided if individuals would remember two words: personal responsibility.

Made in Tropicana

Western Cultures have become victims of their own success. Point of Sale inventory systems dominate our supermarkets to the point where we no longer know where our food comes from. Many people do not know that an egg actually comes from a chicken or that most oranges are grown in Brazil, Florida, or California. The sad reality is that there are actually people that believe oranges are only grown in a place called Tropicana.

On a recent trip to England, I was told of a teacher that tried to teach her students of the cycle of life. Her lecture was to show the children the life of a chicken. She let the class witness an egg under a heat lamp for a period time before the baby chick broke the shell and hatched. The class then fed the baby chick until it became a full grown chicken. Her next plan was to take the grown chicken to the local butcher for killing and processing. Although I have heard conflicting versions of the next events, it became the center of national controversy. People were accusing the teacher of being cruel to animals and trying to inflict mental harm on the children. The teacher had to apologize or face termination. The children were programmed to believe that chicken comes from the supermarket and anyone telling them any different were simply out to traumatize them. So rather than offend the few, the bureaucrats in England chose tell a lie to the many. What will this next generation of kids do when we the people of western civilization face the next major crisis such as the next world war? During world war two, many school children in England were sent to the country side to work at farms. If a national crisis of this magnitude happens again in England, I fear for the welfare of the children there because of the short-sightedness of their elders. The children will have been brought to believe that the government will take care of their every need in an emergency and that food just magically appears at their local ASDA. (Walmart)

Natural Medicine

Even though I used England as an example, the same nonsense thinking is permeating the hearts and minds in the United States. Native cultures, alternative doctors and herbalists around the world both agree that there are certain foods found in nature that can cure the human body of numerous ailments. Yet, we let a corrupt medical system tell us that drugs from the pharmaceutical industry is the only way to treat our bodies. For centuries people have been known to eat cinnamon for diabetic symptoms, mint for digestion, marijuana for glaucoma, limes for scurvy, and garlic for blood cleansing. The list of foods that cure will be to long for me to list so I suggest you talk to your local herbalist or health food practitioner. My point is that we need to arm ourselves with the knowledge of foods and herbs that can treat our bodies effectively in the event modern medicine becomes unavailable or obscenely expensive. Do not let the pharmaceutical industry brainwash your family into thinking that they know what's best for you health when the reality is they only know what is best for their corporate bank accounts. God has given us access to thousands of herbs, plants, and seeds to treat our bodies. Now is a great time to familiarize ourselves with the proper uses and applications of them before the next major crisis hits.

And God said, Behold, I have given you every herb bearing seed, which is upon the face of all the earth, and every tree, in the which is the fruit of a tree yielding seed; to you it shall be for meat. (Genesis 1:29)

Do you have food stored away for emergencies?

Maybe I should start this section by asking a more direct question. My mission is to educate and inform the 350 million people living in the United States that a food crisis that rivaled the first "Great Depression" will be hitting the United States and it will have an adverse effect on its trading partners like Canada and England. This will be partly due to an international financial crisis and the next world war. If your local supermarkets closed down right now, can you honestly feed your family for an extended period of time? Two weeks? A month? Perhaps even a year?

The 'Great Depression' was a period (1929-1939) in United States History when business was poor and many people were out of work. The Great Depression began in October 1929, when the stock market in the United States dropped rapidly. Thousands of investors lost large sums of money and many were wiped out, losing everything. The 'crash' led us into the Great Depression. The ensuing period ranked as the longest and worst period of high unemployment and low business activity in modern times. Banks, stores, and factories were closed and left millions of Americans jobless, homeless, and penniless. Many people came to depend on the government or charity to provide them with food. Researchers have discovered that an estimated 7 million people in the United States starved to death during this low point in American history. However, the actual number of deaths may be 10 million people due to the influx of undocumented immigrants.

According to the September 2014 article in the Wall Street Journal, writer Neil Shah points out that there 46.2 million Americans currently on food stamps even though the number has declined from 47.8 million. Either way you slice it, those numbers are actually alarming. Furthermore, David John Marotta* of the highly respected Marotta Wealth Management group points out that the actual unemployment rate of Americans not working is 37.2% rather than the government figures of 6.7%. Meanwhile the president of TechnoMetrica Market Intelligence, Raghavan Mayur, says the actual U.S. unemployment rate is over 22%. Although I am not a markets expert like these two gentlemen, my research has discovered that they are part of growing list of market professionals that have discovered the dishonesty coming out of Washington D.C. in regards to our supposed economic recovery.**

My point for bringing this up is if we have a repeat of the same governmental policies that led to the first Great Depression, then we can be sure to expect the same results. A major financial depression rears its ugly head first, and then a major world war follows immediately after. So what does this have to with food you may ask? Everything. Back in the days of the first Great Depression 30% of Americans lived on farms. The problem lurks within the numbers of mouths to feed within the confines of the United States versus the amount of farms that produce food. According to the U.S. census, there were 6,288,648 farms within the country on April 1, 1930. As of the year 2012, there remains 2,109,363 farms within the United States. Since one in three U.S. farm products is planted for export, should we recognize all the farms listed from the government data for total food producing farms? Whether you agree with my assertion or not, the total population of the country is now an estimated 319,000,000 people and that does not include the illegal aliens or shall I say "undocumented" people. However, the census for 1930 informs us that there were an estimated 123,000,000 people in the United States. So, if my logic is still working correctly, the United States now has less farms but almost triple the amount of people as opposed to the era of the 1930s.***

    The naysayer will argue that our farming methods are much more productive. I say that depends on your farm's dependence of commercial fertilizers, gasoline, genetically modified foods, etc. Juxtapose that with the fact that some of the political leaders in Washington, sit as board members for agricultural corporations like Monsanto; a company that sells fertilizers and genetically modified seeds.

    The reality without the conspiracy is that the United States is actually a sitting duck for a food crisis to occur. If there is a financial meltdown due to the weakness of the U.S. dollar, the price of gas and oil can skyrocket. Therefore the cost to transport the food around the country in the big semi-trucks will no longer be a cost efficient venture for the corporations involved. Compound this factor with mass riots occurring around the country and the possibilities for social disorder become endless.

    Remember what I said earlier about World War 3? In this day and age most military planners agree that you must strike a country's infrastructure. The United States is so big that it will take too much time and resources to effectively knock out our electric power stations, bridges, railways, and airports. Unless, of course, you use an electromagnetic pulse or EMP for short. One blast from an EMP weapon in our atmosphere could put America back 100 years because of the damage to our infrastructure. The weapon could literally fry the circuits of all the electronic devices in the country and this includes our electric power stations. How will we have food transported if the electric run gas pumps will not work? How will stores refrigerate the food if the electricity is out for 6 months or more? (FYI-Congress is aware of this threat but has blocked the funding to protect our electric grid from this type of attack. But cheer up, they approved the funding to fight ISIS, ISIL, Al Queda, Ukraine rebels, etc.)

Is storing extra food and provisions biblical?

Of course it is! Let me name a few people from the bible: Noah, Joseph, the widow of Zarapeth, the King of Judah (during Elijah's ministry), and the apostles from the New Testament. These folks can considered the "original" preppers.

That last example I mentioned is the one I like to present to the Christian that absolutely refuses to prepare for anything. I have to do that with Christians because they will quickly point out that the other references were from the Old Testament of the bible therefore under the old law. The New Testament disciples were preppers according to the book of Acts, because it says:

27And in these days came prophets from Jerusalem unto Antioch.
28And there stood up one of them named Agabus, and signified by the spirit that there should be great dearth throughout all the world: which came to pass in the days of Claudius Caesar.
29Then the disciples, every man according to his ability, determined to send relief unto the brethren which dwelt in Judaea:

(Acts 11:27-29)

The word dearth as used in verse 28 is the old English word for famine. Although the reasons for the famine tend to vary depending on the scholar, there was a food shortage around the period of 46 A.D. The Roman Empire went as far North as the British Isles to the hot deserts of the Middle East. There was massive starvation due to this famine and this occurred after the resurrection of Jesus Christ. The same way God warned Joseph to store food for Egypt, God warned the New Testament believers to store food for Judea. If the Christians on the scene sent relief to there church members living in Judea, isn't it safe to say they had stored up some provisions to help the not so fortunate? It's incredible the amount of churches that I encounter that refuse to prepare for any emergencies when the people in the bible seemed to have an emergency preparedness mindset. A tradition and biblical mandate is to bless the poor. When crisis hits an area, the people normally come to the church for help. Here is a news flash for those of you that consider yourself "Christian"; you are the church. If things hit the fan in your area, be ready to help someone in need. By showing the actions of Christ, these folks may be willing to receive him in their hearts.

If you are a member of a church organization with able bodied church members that live in the United States yet they refuse to prepare for the coming famine, then I highly suggest praying for them everyday. However I will interject, if they are indeed baptized with the Holy Spirit, then they should have the gifts of miracles working through them with more efficiency. I highly expect these brothers and sisters that are truly filled with the Holy Spirit to perform numerous kinds of miracles including multiplying food when necessary. From my point of view, the key to making the best decisions towards the future is to be balanced. Proof of this balance was in the book Acts (11:28-29). Peter and Paul aided the prophet Agabus with the supplying of food for the brothers and sisters in Judea. These 3 prophets were all filled with the Holy Spirit and they each demonstrated different miracles such as prophesying (predicting the future), supernatural healings, speaking in tongues, and raising people from the dead. However, there is no biblical account of God telling them to multiply food during the relief effort of the great famine of 46 AD. I think it's because God wanted teach all of the new followers of Jesus the most important thing: To love each other as you would yourself. You have to pardon me because this is what is called divine revelation. Imagine being in a situation where there is no food to be found any where, and some guys that claim they are followers of "Jesus of Nazareth", show up to your house and give your family a free bag of groceries. They simply tell you that "Jesus loves you" and they leave. At some point you would want to know who loves you that much to have his followers drop off some food supplies to keep your poor family from starving. If you know any preppers that considers themselves Christians, perhaps you should enlighten them on this verse:

15If a brother or sister be naked, and destitute of daily food,
16And one of you say unto them, Depart in peace, be ye warmed and filled; notwithstanding ye give them not those things which are needful to the body; what doth it profit?
(James 2:15-16)

The Crop Flop

Many preppers would prefer to be self sufficient. Self sufficient simply refers to people that can survive and flourish with little or no help from the outside world. Extreme cases would be certain people that live in the most remote parts of the world whether it be an Eskimo or a tribe deep in the Amazon jungle. In the United States, there are few Native American tribes that remain self-sufficient as well as certain religious groups like the Amish.

The one thing I admire from all of the self sufficient people I encounter around the world is there ability to adapt to changing situations in nature. These cultures normally pass down the teachings of adaptation to every new generation. A Massi warrior in Africa knows exactly how to adjust his cattle if there is a hungry lion lurking nearby. The Native Americans knew exactly how to adjust their farming techniques during a season of drought to still have provisions for the winter. However, many folks in the preparedness community do not have this knowledge. They spend money on "survival seeds", but they won't even grow a tomato plant in a flower pot. Many preppers think planting a garden is as easy dropping a seed in the ground, and they couldn't be more uninformed. They need to acquire growing knowledge and plan for the seed to flourish. If you think your going to be able to start tilling the land for growing food when the major crisis hits your country, I feel it's my duty to let you know that your partially fooling yourself. Farming takes time and practice; even on a small scale. For example:

Do you know what time of year is best to plant your seeds?

Will there be too much sun where you are planting them?

Will you have enough water available to water the seeds and potential garden?

Will the wildlife such as birds or deer feast on your garden?

Which method will you use to get rid of them? (A scarecrow does not work on every bird and they do not work on deer.)

Will your garden be visible to hungry people? (History proves if there is mass chaos in a country, starvation and theft became the norm.)

What is the growing cycle for the area you live in? (For example: The growing cycle in Augusta, Georgia is totally different than Peekskill, New York.)

It is this lack of generational wisdom that will doom thousands of people by means of starvation. This will be a reality in the technologically rich United States if the power grid ever goes down or a devastating economic collapse. But there are solutions to avoid starvation on both the natural front and the spiritual front.

On the natural front I highly suggest you seek knowledge pertaining to gardening and farming. If you are one of the people reading this book that has space for a garden but you do not have the physical strength to work the land, let me introduce you to "Rick Austin, the Survivalist Gardener". He is the author of **Secret Garden of Survival- How to grow a Camouflaged Food-Forest**. His book shows you how to make a nutrient rich garden without the application of back breaking work. In addition to less work, his book also teaches you how to disguise your garden from thieves and marauders. A highly important lesson if we can expect massive food shortages in the United States.

If you are serious about growing your food I suggest you observe your surroundings to see what type of food production methods you can acquire. If you live in an apartment, check out hydroponics or bucket gardening from your balcony. Maybe you can start your own garden on the top of the building. I suggest asking the building superintendent for permission to access the area and promise him some fresh veggies for his cooperation. If you live in a house, check the amount of space you can use for a garden. Perhaps you should check the garage space as well. I recently met an elderly lady in North Carolina that grew a fruit bearing lemon tree in her garage, so please do not tell me these things are hard or impossible. In your spare time, begin to explore the gardens people are creating at home on Youtube. There are some really creative people whose videos give you the instructions and ideas for absolutely free. One gentleman in Arizona has created a self sustaining food garden inside his empty swimming pool as well as self sustaining fish farm. He produces enough food weekly to feed his family as well as immediate neighbors. We all wish we had a guy like that in our family!

Spiritual Food

Self sufficiency can be a really cool thing in this day and age, especially when it comes to growing your own food. I advise people to make relationships with independent growers and farms because in the future, your ability to get fresh produce will be worth its weight in gold. However, it will always be your priceless relationship with God that will secure your family food supply.

Many farmers and small time gardeners have experienced blight on their produce. When I ask a prepper that plans on starting a farm, they are normally clueless to the term. Blights can be an organism (insect or a fungus) that leaves plants withered and destroyed. When a blight occurs, it can literally affect thousands of people if the entire crop for a community is destroyed. My friend, Pastor Charlie Reed of North Carolina, witnessed this dreadful phenomena as a child. His father was a farmer that was struggling to keep the bank from seizing his plot of land. To make matters worse, the struggling farmer got word of some kind of blight destroying the farmers crops throughout Western North Carolina, and Northern Georgia. The prospect of becoming homeless did not sit well with Charlie's dad. In a final act of defiance and faith, Charlie's dad sat his son on his shoulders and walked out onto his farm land. He walked over the entire farm and intersected every row of cabbage. Little Charlie heard his Dad get louder with every step as he walked through the large plot of land. It wasn't before long Charlie realized that his father was praying over every cabbage that was planted on the property. To this day Charlie remembers some of the actual prayers that came from his father's mouth:

"And I will rebuke the devourer for your sakes and he shall not destroy the fruits of your ground; neither shall your vine cast her

fruit before the time in the field, saith the Lord of hosts. (Malachi 3:11)

"The Lord is my shepherd, I shall not want." (Psalm 23:1)

"Goodness and mercy shall follow me all the days of my life:" (Psalm 23:6)

Young Charlie and his dad eventually went inside the house believing God for the impossible. Weeks went by and the news of the blight affecting farmers throughout the region carried like wildfire. Entire crops were being lost and many farmers ended up losing their farm land. Meanwhile, Charlie's house was in a state of euphoria. Charlie's dad was the only farmer in the region whose crops reached full maturity! His harvest of cabbage and other vegetables were healthy and vibrant. The Reed family farm produced a bumper crop during a famine.

Dry Faith?

The story I previously mentioned is not an isolated incident. God honors faith in survival situations including droughts. A lack of rain to modern farmers is bad for business and to a prepper, it can mean life or death in the future. Some preppers believe they can grow an abundance of food in a survival crisis. However, one season of drought can ruin the growing season of even the most prepared. Your best preparation for your garden, farm or homestead is to have the presence of God on your property. In1998 a man named Angus Buchan wrote a book called **Faith Like Potatoes**, which was later turned into a Hollywood movie. It was based on a remarkable true story of a white farmer becoming a Pastor in South Africa. The farmer had to deal with racial tensions, language barriers, and worst of all, a lack of rain. A major drought comes to the region and the major scientists considered the growing season to be a loss. The Pastor/Farmer was told by the scientists as well as the indigenous people of the area to avoid growing food due to the drought;

especially potatoes. Considering the dry conditions, it seemed like logical advice from everyone. Low on finances, but high on faith, the Pastor/Farmer ignores everyone and plants potatoes in the dry dirt. However, he prayed constantly for God to bless his farm. The end result was the farm yielding a bumper crop of massive sized healthy potatoes!

Reality Check

Well, some of you might say, "Pastor, I don't have that problem where I live because the rainfall is always steady."

My reply to that statement would be, "That's great. Now how do you stop all the animals and humans from stealing your food from your garden?"

The last statement is a reality check for my self sufficient friends reading this book. When you have a healthy garden or farm with plenty of food, it will attract four legged animals. If the hunger crisis gets that bad, be prepared for the two legged animals. Most people have not developed the mindset to camouflage their garden from roving mobs of people. If it's a large farm you will need security guards to protect the food. But if you have a relationship with Jesus Christ, you may not need anything extra to protect your food supply except prayer.

My late mentor John Perault had a mini-farm on his homestead in North Carolina. Since he understood the dangers of mobs coming to steal food, he chose to have his homestead deep in the mountains of Western Carolina. With a low population in his vicinity, he was growing a litany of healthy organic foods every year. However, he had a growing problem for his mini farm. It seemed as if the animals were sending each other text messages for the free buffet. The animals were visiting his massive garden every passing year and bring new friends with them every time. First it was the squirrels, then the birds, then the rabbits, then the groundhogs, and then finally the deer. With wild boar and black bears in the area, John got fed up. He was not going to move from his home because the animals were eating his family's survival garden. John walked into his garden one day prayed this prayer, "Father, I know you made the animals and you made the food in my garden, but can you please send your animals to eat somewhere else. This food is for my family and friends, especially for when the tough times come."

To my knowledge, that prayer was said years ago and the animals have not come to eat since it was prayed. It's almost like there is a giant "do not enter" sign that only animals can see. The only people that eat the food from the mini-farm is John's friends and family. The way John Perault intended it to be!

I can hear some of you guys reading the book saying, "That's just a coincidence. The animals found a new farm to raid. Besides, the tough times are not here yet. Those friends will be stealing from the farm in a crisis."

My answer to that is to stop being fearful and have faith. God is still in the miracle business! There may be a time when the food is low and there are too many mouths to feed. Instead of acting like the devil we should try our best to imitate Christ. The next story reminds me of the car bumper sticker that says: What would Jesus do?

These type of miracles are common occurrences in certain third world countries where starvation is the norm. My friend Pastor Emmanuel Twagirimana and his wife Isabelle witnessed a divine food drop in Africa. The couple went to a remote area outside of Rwanda to preach at a small church. When the church service was over, Pastor Emmanuel was shocked to see there was not enough food to feed the 30 people in attendance. There was enough rice in the pot to feed maybe 6 people if he stretched it. He was grieved in his spirit to know that some of these people were going to walk miles to get home on en empty stomach. The Pastor and his wife covered the pot of rice and began to pray. As they prayed, they continually thanked God for feeding all of the people at the meeting. They uncovered the pot and the amount looked the same. However, as they began to share the food out to people, it supernaturally shared out to thirty plates. God actually confirmed the miracle by allowing the people to get a second share by the time the service was over!

"We walk by faith, not by sight."
(2 Corinthians 5:7)

Sources

*http://www.washingtonexaminer.com/wall-street-adviser-actual-unemployment-is-37.2-misery-index-worst-in-40-years/article/2542604

**http://www.dailyfinance.com/2010/07/16/what-is-the-real-unemployment-rate/

***http://www.agcensus.usda.gov/Publications/2012/Preliminary_Report/Highlights.pdf

Chapter 3

Hypocrite or Hypochondriac?

I like using older dictionaries to find the meaning of words because I find the definitions to be more truthful and less politically correct. According to my 1828 edition of the Noah Webster dictionary the word hypocrite still paints a colorful picture:

Hypocrite – 1. One who feigns to be what he is not; one who has the form of godliness without the power, or who assumes an appearance of piety and virtues, when he is destitute of true religion. 2. A dissembler; one who assumes a false appearance.

On the other hand, the word hypochondriac has changed meanings over the years. In 1828, the word was defined:

Hypochondriac – A person affected with debility, lowness of spirits or melancholy.

Yet, in the year 2015 numerous dictionaries define the word hypochondriac as:

A person who is abnormally anxious about their health.

What do these words have to do with prepping? Not much, but be careful of prepping with such a person. In the previous chapter I mentioned the scenario of the wealthy Christian with the fully stocked bomb shelter and his poor Christian neighbor that could only afford rice and beans. I believe the correct answer to the question in the previous chapter is, "What would Jesus do?" Okay, that is too easy for my critics because they will simply say, "Jesus wouldn't need a bomb shelter because he would bring peace to the world!" Let me replace the answer with a series of questions built along the same lines. What would the apostles Peter and Paul do? What would Mother Theresa do? What would Martin Luther King Jr. do? What would Ghandi do? I believe they would pray for a miracle first. If the miracle didn't happen, then they would try their best to fit every one in the shelter starting with the children first. If that couldn't happen, then they would give up there spot for one of the neighbor's children. How far will you go to help others especially for those of you reading this claiming to be a Christian? Jesus said, "Greater love hath no man than this, that a man lay down his life for his friends." (John 15:13)

The amount of preppers I run into that will let their neighbor starve to death is mind boggling. Don't get me wrong, I always advise discretion and wisdom in the numerous scenarios you may encounter in the future because the bible teaches us to be "wise like serpents". However, Jesus taught us that it is more blessed to give than it is to receive. Instead of purchasing a bomb shelter for my wife and kids, I decided its more important to have extra essentials for my immediate neighbors should the need arise. Even though some of my neighbors are not preparedness minded, I still plan on showing them attributes of Jesus Christ during a crisis. I can tell someone that God is love, but showing them His love is more important.

Pure religion and undefiled before God and the Father is this, To visit the fatherless and widows in their affliction, and to keep himself unspotted from the world. (James 1:26)

In the future, you may need to remember this verse to keep yourself from becoming the definition of a hypocrite. Let me give you an example of what I mean. A few years ago, I met a prepper named Mike at the Atlanta gun show. He basically said if all hell breaks loose in America tomorrow, he would shoot anyone that stepped onto his property. I had to ask Mike if he was sure that he was a "Christian". Cleary offended at my question he tried to justify the reasons why he has the right to shoot the person dead. Then I simply asked Mike, "Suppose it's a ten year old kid foraging for food and water because both of his parents have died in the disaster?" Instead of becoming a blessing to the orphan, Mike was more than willing to become the curse. Mike was being a hypocrite because he also claimed he was a Christian. I can tell you with all authority brothers and sisters, killing an innocent human being is a deplorable act before God. Please exercise restraint and caution in all situations.

I have met some preppers that claim they are of the Christian faith but their actions have shown otherwise. Jesus said it best when he said, "You will know them by their fruits." The hypocrite and the hypochondriac are two colorful characters you will find in the preparedness movement. The hypochondriac in the preparedness movement thinks that everything he comes across is designed to kill or maim him so he must make preparations to stop the threat. In many cases the hypochondriac prepper will try to examine a local problem with a global solution or vice versa. For example, I knew a self described "survivalist prepper" that developed a rather nasty cough and sinus pressure. He was convinced that it was from the chemical trails being sprayed from the overhead commercial airplanes. Even though he did not know the actual difference between a cumulus cloud, a com trail from a jet liner, and an actual chemical trail in the sky, he would say his runny nose is from inhaling chemicals sprayed over head from airplanes to sicken the population. I am not saying that it is impossible but I quickly pointed out to this gentleman that we are in the beginning of spring and it's because of all the pollen in the air. My second dosage of logic came by observing his immediate friends and family. They were all healthy and showed no symptoms of any kind. This gentleman became the prisoner of his own reality.

Here is another story of a hypochondriac prepper. This gentleman I know was working as a sales clerk at a local Walmart in North Carolina. On one particular day he came to work with a surgical dust mask, latex gloves, and a bottle of hand sanitizer. I observed his obsessive use of the hand sanitizer after every new customer left his checkout area. (Yes, he would use hand sanitizer while wearing his latex gloves!) Since I knew him personally I decided to use his aisle during checkout. When I asked him why he had on the surgical mask and other paraphernalia, he quietly reminded me of the growing swine flu epidemic. At the time, there were no confirmed cases of swine flu in our state or the neighboring state. However, there were reports of normal flu deaths. So he basically spread fear and paranoia at his job in this tiny North Carolina town. Eventually the manager reduced his hours until he stopped wearing the fearful outfit. Granted, if there was indeed proof of the swine flue permeating the area, I think the young man would have a valid argument for wearing the additional protection. Since there wasn't any cases of swine flu in our area, he fell into the category of another hypochondriac prepper.

These are small examples of the hypochondriac type preppers. I point them out because you should be extremely careful of them. These are the ones that make the entire preparedness community look bad. They often times will panic at the first sign of bad news and are proven to be untrustworthy in sound decision making skills. Many of them are possessed by a spirit of fear instead a spirit of wisdom. I argue, that these people will try to outrun their shadow on a bright sunny day.

A double minded man is unstable in all his ways.
(James 1:8)

As for the hypocrite prepper, I noticed that there are two different types of them because one deals with religion meanwhile the other deals with politics. The first type of hypocrite prepper in my humble opinion, is the one that will continually participate in activities or behavior that is contrary to the teachings of Jesus Christ. For example, I know of a bible teacher that teaches preparedness in the physical and the spiritual realm. Yet he overlooked his teachings when he decided to have an affair with another man's wife. He then had the audacity to claim that the people who believed the horrible rumor were mentally unstable. The hypocritical bible teacher was eventually caught red handed by his wife and his ministry was shut down.

The second type of hypocrite prepper is the one that will continually participate in activities and behavior that will harm their fellow man but would not approve of those behaviors and activities being done to themselves or their loved ones. Many, but not all, politicians in the United States fall into this category because they will make laws against the hoarding of food and ammunition but they are the ones with the private access to underground bunkers dispersed across the United States to protect themselves and their immediate families should the need arise. The legendary Greenbrier hotel in West Virginia proves my point. This luxury hotel is the site of a massive underground bomb shelter built for the United States congress in the event of nuclear war with Russia during the Cold War. It was equipped with a litany of survival goods including food, guns, ammunition, and medicine. The government decided to shut it down when the location of the secret complex got leaked to the public by the Washington Post newspaper in 1992. (If the Cuban Missile Crisis occurred in 1962, why was this facility still in use some 30 years later?)

A few years ago, I met a U.S. Senator at a church luncheon. Out of respect, I will not name him, but he kindly sat at the table with me and about five older businessmen. Since I was the youngest guy in the group and the only African American at the table, I kept my mouth closed and listened more. As he posed to be one of the boys, we were able to discuss all different topics with him. We jokingly chatted about cars, sports, and the politics of marriage. The conversation somehow veered into serious topics likes terrorism and economic collapse. As some of the men brought up worse case scenarios, I simply studied the politician's body language. When the reality of social collapse entered the conversation, I said the following words to the Senator:

"At least you won't have to worry about this stuff, the government will have you whisked away into some bunker some where while the rest of us fight it out."

The Senator responded: "Well I wouldn't just leave my wife. I would have to make sure she is...."

At that moment he stopped mid sentence. He realized that he told a secret without telling the secret. The men sitting with me saw right through his "I am one of the boys routine". The men in Washington D.C. would like us to believe that their preparedness measures are done for the "continuity of government" when the reality is they are more interested in saving their own skin.

Today in 2015, I have been informed through various channels including retired military, that there are numerous underground bunkers built for high ranking politicians and wealthy corporate executives scattered throughout the United States equipped with luxuries such as movie theatres and health gyms. Like the Greenbrier hotel in West Virginia, many of these facilities are built with funneled tax payer money, however the common American people do not have any such place to run to in the event of a massive war or natural disaster. The American public has a few minor facilities but they are quite comical compared to the ones used by elected officials. Ironically, under recent guidelines from the Department of Homeland Security, private citizens can be labeled a "potential" terrorist for having the same items as the politicians that supposedly serve you. Do you see the hypocrisy with these types of preppers?

If you live in the United States, write or call your elected representative in Washington D.C. and tell them to do two things:

1) Stop making hypocritical laws against their fellow citizens
2) Stop making hypocritical laws to antagonize nuclear armed countries.

By doing these two things, our hypocritical government officials would not need to build underground bunkers to protect themselves from anarchy or nuclear war.

Here is a deeper issue with hypocrisy among preppers in high levels of government. The Israeli government has always spent money on bunkers and civil defense for their populace. Many of the citizens there are knowledgeable of the use of guns and the government encourages the citizens to have provisions set aside in case of a surprise attack by a neighboring country. Lately, the Russian government has been building their civil defense infrastructure, namely bomb shelters to protect their citizens in case of nuclear war. These places are being built around their country, stocked with emergency provisions and the ability to hold millions of people. I can not speak for the UK or Canada, but the closest thing we have here in the United Sates may be internment camps. The problems with internment camps are too many to entertain in this book, but I suggest you ask any Japanese American that was sent to one during World War Two. Lets just say the similarities between an internment camp and a high security prison are quite shocking.*

One thing remains certain: God is quite aware of these high ranking politicians and wealthy globalists that think they can hide out in underground bunkers and escape judgments for their evil doings. According to the last book in the bible, the book of Revelation tells of the sheer horror these individuals face when they realize that their super secret taxpayer funded underground bunkers are useless in protecting them from God's divine judgment upon them:

15And the kings of the earth, and the great men, and the rich men, and the chief captains, and the mighty men, and every bondman, and every free man, hid themselves in the dens and in the rocks of the mountains;
16And said to the mountains and rocks, Fall on us, and hide us from the face of him that sitteth on the throne, and from the wrath of the Lamb:
17For the great day of his wrath is come; and who shall be able to stand?

Revelation 6:15-17

Sources

*http://rt.com/news/prime-time/moscow-bomb-shelters-outskirts/

Chapter 4

Cash for Gold Or The Cash Cajole?

Let me begin this chapter of the book by telling you that I have been buying and selling precious metals for a number of years. I have always loved the appearance of gold and silver. So it wasn't by accident that as I began to study the bible, I noticed the importance of the two metals. I figured that if God would pave his streets with the stuff and put it inside his living room, these shiny fellas must have some kind of earth shattering importance. However, I also noticed that God never used dollars to decorate his neighborhood.

If you ever read a bible, you will notice that gold and silver is mentioned from the beginning of the book (Genesis) all the way until the end (Revelation). Even during the post apocalyptic era in the book of Revelation, there are still references to the stuff. I believe the metals hold a value simply because God designed them to. Whether they are used for currency, jewelry, or industry, these precious metals will have a use. Think about it every time you see a home with solar panels on the roof.

It is no secret that many Americans are waking up to the fact that the United States is in serious financial trouble. Even though the mainstream media continues to bombard the public with manipulated numbers for the economic recovery, many of the brightest minds from Wall Street are beginning to warn us of an economic collapse or a possible default of the U.S. dollar. This would have a devastating impact on financial markets around the world. Is this even possible?

Let's look at the facts:

The national debt is currently 17 trillion dollars and expanding everyday. At some point, our international trading partners will begin to view the U.S. dollar as toilet paper because our Federal Reserve keeps printing it with reckless abandonment.*

When combined together, the governments of China and Japan hold about 3 trillion dollars of our United States debt. If the Chinese or Japanese government stops purchasing our debt we will have no choice but to default. Please keep in mind that China has been publicly stating their desire to use the Yuan as the world's reserve currency. The Chinese Central bank has been buying up large amounts of gold and silver bullion from around the world. To become the world's number one reserve currency, one must have silver and gold to back the currency. **

The average life for fiat (paper) currency is 40 years. Well some of you readers may argue that we have been using paper currency in the United States for over 40 years. Have we really? For the sake of time, I highly suggest that you research Richard Nixon's decision to take the United States off the gold standard in 1971 and the role his decision has played in dollar debasement, recessions, and currency manipulations.

The Federal Reserve is a privately run bank. The name Federal Reserve was given to this cartel to hoodwink the public into thinking it was an original part of our federal government. However, the reality is the Federal Reserve is no more Federal than Federal Express. Some of the owners of this bank are foreign nationals who have no allegiance or loyalty to the American people.

So what does this mean to you preppers around the world?

If you are preparing for economic Armageddon, gold and silver have historically been proven to preserve the wealth of the rich and poor. It has been used as a means of exchange for thousands of years and it will continuously outlast any fiat currency.

Let me give you this colorful explanation. If a bank robber stole some paper money from any country in the world and buried it; what would happen if he came back to get his money in 100 years? The money would have rotted is the first thing most people say! However, let us examine this case closely. If he would try to spend the money he would realize that value of the money is worthless due to inflation, or that the government in question has ceased to exist. I challenge you to go to any country in the world and try to use their 100 year old paper money at the store in their local economy. You will be laughed out of the store or maybe even arrested! Suppose the robber had stolen gold or silver coins and returned 100 years later to spend them? He would be able to go to most countries in the world and exchange them for whatever paper or digital currency that is being used while earning a handsome profit. He would also have the option of trading or bartering them with business owners or every day people for the things he needed.

Life Saving Uses

Have you ever heard of colloidal silver? It is the medical industries arch enemy in the world of antibiotics. Amazingly simply to produce, many Americans are learning to make it within the confines of their own home. By simply using a pure ounce of silver and some easy to find equipment, you can have one of nature's strongest antibiotics at your disposal within hours. This is my reason for investing in one ounce silver rounds: Protection from inflation and protection from bacteria.

During World War II, Adolf Hitler ordered his army to round up Jewish people, gypsies, and any other person he deemed undesirable. Many of these people were forced into labor camps or exterminated. However, not every one of Hitler's soldiers was willing to kill an innocent human being. Some resisted out of a sense of conscience but others denied the killing orders because of one word: greed.

I have read countless stories about Nazi soldiers that accepted bribes from people to let a Jewish family escape into hiding or turn a blind eye during a security checkpoint. Many soldiers and local police would facilitate bribes with people looking to escape Hitler's occupied areas. The medium of exchange always seemed to be gold. It was common for a Jewish father to break his gold chain into pieces to pay any bribe necessary to help his love ones get to freedom. Sadly to say, I envision such days coming to the United States of America where foreign troops are being bribed by Americans to avoid going to prison camps. Similar events are happening right now in some parts of the Middle East!

Inflation Protection

Who has ever played a game of Russian roulette and lived to tell about it? Not too many people. For those of you not familiar with the game Russian roulette, you simply put a bullet into the chamber of a revolver, spin the chamber, point the revolver at your head and pull the trigger. There is generally a 1 in 6 chance you will pull the trigger and a bullet will be fired. The end of the game for this player is usually permanent.

As this book hits bookstores across America, world leaders are playing the same game with the U.S. dollar and the meal table of every American in the country. The brain surgeons in Washington DC decided to force the American people into their game of Russian roulette by starting sanctions against Russia for their involvement with the Ukraine situation. As a response to the United States threat, the Russian government has warned the world that if the United States begins to sanction Russia, they will dump all of their holdings of U.S. dollars and collapse the economy of the United States. In theory, if the Russians begin dumping U.S. dollars, hyperinflation will take place in the United States. Many financial analysts say it could not happen, but what if they are wrong? What if China decides to join Russia in the fray? If it does happen, many of the items we pay for in retail shops across America will begin to quadruple in price. Imagine paying $15 for a loaf of bread, $20 for some milk and $500 to fill your car with gas?

You probably are wondering what this has to do with buying silver and gold. Silver and gold are the best ways to protect your assets from the scourge of hyperinflation. As the dollar gets dumped by international power broker's like Russia and China, the price of silver and gold will make a steady climb upward. A person with a savings account of lets say $100,000 will wake up to the reality that his savings account is only worth $20,000. However, a person with $20,000 worth of gold and silver could theoretically be worth $100,000. Regardless of the exact financial figure, the latter person will have preserved his wealth.

This particular episode has played out in many nations across the world when investors have lost confidence in a nation's fiat (paper) currency and this is exactly what the Russians are banking on! Back in the year 1919, Germany had its financial system experience hyperinflation thus weakening the strength of the German Mark. The currency became so weak that people had to bring a suitcase filled with cash to purchase a loaf of bread. Only the citizens that saw the economic tsunami coming purchased gold to ride the wave of uncertainty. They witnessed their ounce of gold trading at 170 marks in January 1919 and then skyrocketing to a value of 87 trillion marks by November 1923. The people that had invested in physical gold were able to provide themselves with a decent living meanwhile other Germans simply starved to death.

My sister's dream is America's nightmare!

Back in 2010, I felt it was my duty to warn my sisters in my immediate family about the coming storms heading to the United States. My sister Karen was living on the outskirts of New York City in city called Yonkers. A successful realtor, she became intrigued about the things I told her regarding America's financial future. She is perhaps one of my most "street smart" relatives so you can always speak to her as a layman and not as a pastor. After hearing my views on the demise of the U.S. dollar, she told me she is going to pray about it. I returned to North Carolina and continued with my normal activities.

A week or so passed since I was in New York and I received a phone call from Karen. She told me of the scariest dreams she has ever had. Karen shared the following with me:

"I was walking through different areas of New York City and the city was almost a ghost town. There were people still there but not as many cars on the road and not as many lights. People were clearly struggling to make ends meet and poverty was everywhere. Since it was cold, I walked over to a few people warming themselves over a garbage can fire. I put my hands over the fire to keep warm and to my surprise, the people were using dollar bills for the fire. The money was absolutely worthless!"

1) Go to now, ye rich men, weep and howl for your miseries that shall come upon you.

2) Your riches are corrupted, and your garments are moth eaten.

3) Your gold and silver is cankered; and the rust of them shall be a witness against you, and shall eat your flesh as it were fire. Ye have heaped treasure together for the last days.

James 5 (1-3)

When man divides, God still provides!

Some of you reading this may be saying, "Brother Keith, I know what your saying about gold and silver is true, but I can barely afford to pay attention. Even my bills now have bills. Is there any hope for the person that can not afford to purchase silver and gold?"

Absolutely! The purpose of this book is to bring hope and wisdom: not fear. The word of God says "Christ in you the hope of glory.." You are going to be one of the people that God will supernaturally provide help for. If you are walking honestly with God in your life and doing your best to live by his word, then you will be on top of his "miracle list". Let me tell you the story of my darkest financial hour.

A few years before I became a pastor and a best selling author, I was your typical traveling salesman and struggling entre-pre-negro. I had recently moved from Florida to North Carolina with my wife and young son. It was a difficult time in my life because I was living in a new state with barely any friends and family. My wife tended to my son while I was trying to keep a roof over our head. Although I would work any odd job I could find, my main source of income would come from selling survival products at gun shows in Georgia and North Carolina. It began to seem like there was a black cloud over my life and my wallet. Every time I would hit a monthly financial goal, there would be two unforeseen bills approaching. (By the way, a financial goal was having the rent paid on time.)

It was depressing because it felt like every time I was digging my family out of the financial hole, a dump truck called poverty pulled up and unloaded on me. Even though I tithed and prayed, the bills mounted up like an old Wild West movie. I was selling everything I owned to pay the bills including my gold and silver!

At last, a lifeline showed up! I was hired by company in the Atlanta area as a consultant. The gig was paying $55,000 a year plus benefits so the timing was great considering I was weeks behind on bills. Everything was going great until an employee was trying to get his son hired. Since the company was only hiring 3 new people, he needed to get one of the new guys fired. Guess who fell in the crosshairs of the firing squad? The black dude. (Don't worry, I am not racist, but I couldn't pass on the punchline.) So anyway, I literally ride home crying to God saying, "Why me, big Homey?" I pulled the car into my sister's driveway soaking wet from tears and the broken air conditioner. As I sat there questioning if God even cares about my finances, I noticed a two year old running in the street. If this was your typical, rundown, drug infested neighborhood in Atlanta, I may have just let nature take its course. But my sister lives in an upscale neighborhood on the outskirts of Atlanta so I knew something wasn't right. In horror, I watched the child running toward a busy intersection. That's when I realized my bills and the eviction notice no longer mattered, this kid was about to resemble road kill if I didn't try to save him. Sure enough, I could have beat Usain Bolt for the gold medal that day because I snatched the boy right before he was hit by a car. I eventually found the house he ran out of. His parents didn't know that his older sister opened the door and let her brother go for a run. The mother of the baby had more spiritual sense than me because she waved her hands to the sky and screamed, "Thank you Jesus for sending this man to save my baby!"

Later that evening I had questions that only God could answer. How am I going to pay my bills with eviction looming? How many more personal items do I need to sell to keep a roof over my families head? Should I move back to Miami or New York? Does God even care about my family finances? That night I prayed to God with an attitude.

I said, "Why did you let me come all the way to Atlanta to get fired?"

In a quiet voice, God simply said to me, "What is the price of a child?"

I said, "There is none."

God replies, "Alright then."

It then hit me like a ton of bricks. This entire experience was about being put in the right place at the right time to save a child. God is the greatest chess player in the universe. The devil must have been planning on destroying that child for months, but God in his intelligence used a prepper in financial ruin to save the child's life. Final Score: God 7-The Devil 0

Back to my point. After driving back to North Carolina to my bug out home, my wife told me I had a phone call on the business line. I thought to myself, "Wow, one business call for the entire month." It turns out this customer met me at a gun show months before and they were ready to do business. The customer purchased $10,000 worth of goods from me! (Talk about divine timing!)

Are you a prepper in some serious financial problems? Perhaps you would like to prepare more but your money is lacking? I want you to know that God does care about you and your finances. He is still on the throne and no one can move him! You are probably going through a test right now and your breakthrough is about to come through. If I told you all the times when I was flat on my face financially and God provided a miracle, you will tell me to produce a movie, because the stories sound like they were made for Hollywood.

As preppers, we put a lot of focus on the earthly resources like cash and gold but why not focus on the one who owns all the resources? I support buying gold and silver but we have to keep things in perspective. Not everyone can afford to own silver and gold. But we all can afford to have a relationship with the one who owns all the silver and gold. Would you agree?

"The silver is mine, and the gold is mine, saith the LORD of hosts."
(Haggai 2:8)

Your gold won't save you

The amount of preppers that I meet that think their wealth will save them is in for a rude awakening. When disasters of biblical proportions happen, there are times when money loses all value. This has even happened to silver and gold! Let me give you an example:

When Hurricane Katrina destroyed sections of New Orleans, many people found themselves swimming in water. Their luxury home near the levees was under water and the only thing that mattered was survival. If you owned a boat, and a wealthy business man offered you one million dollars in cash or one million ounces of pure gold; would you accept it? Of course not because you know the boat is key to your survival. You would tell him to keep his money while you attempt to row your family to dry land. Do you think I am being dramatic? The same thing happened in 1912 when people were cruising on a ship called the Titanic. Wealthy business men offered people with access to lifeboats their money and valuable jewelry to have their seat on the lifeboat. Even though they were offered enough money to live off for a year, most people said no to the offers. Still not convincing enough? When Typhoon Haiyan hit the Philippines in 2013, media reports suggested the casualties were near 10,000 people dead meanwhile 1,000,000 were homeless. Areas the size of New Jersey were obliterated by the 200 mile per hour winds. People were left to fend for themselves amid the massive destruction zones. Roaming gangs went to any house that remained standing and robbed them of food and water. The cash and gold were not on the high list of goods for the crooks but immediate survival was. The people living through this hell quickly realized that they could not eat the gold nor could they drink the paper money.

I believe there will be a temporary time to reap the benefits of investing in gold and silver. More or less around the time of financial Armageddon. As major countries dump the dollar or the derivatives markets collapse, the timing of owning gold and silver will be important to any family seeking to preserve their wealth. However, if time repeats itself just like the first great depression in the United States, then we must be ready to face another world war. This war will be fought with much deadlier weapons and the battlefield will engulf the entire northern hemisphere. The weapons used will be strategic nuclear missiles, weaponized flu viruses, and cyber warfare to shut down electric grids. Who is going to trade their gold bars in radioactive fallout? Who is going to accept cash when everyone is catching Ebola like the common flu? Why would I accept your silver coins when I have the food and water? Think about it folks....

Neither their silver nor their gold shall be able to deliver them in the day of the LORD'S wrath; but the whole land shall be devoured by the fire of his jealousy: for he shall make even a speedy riddance of all them that dwell in the land.
(Zephaniah 1:18)

Sources

*http://www.washingtontimes.com/news/2013/oct/18/us-debt-jumps-400-billion-tops-17-trillion-first-t/

** http://www.foxbusiness.com/economy-policy/2015/04/16/japan-owns-more-us-debt-than-china/

Authors Note: The secret to getting out of financial hole is to begin giving. Jesus said "give, and it shall be given unto you." Every time I was in financial ruin I began to bless other people in need and those actions always unlocked a financial door for me.

Chapter 5

Smoke the Rock OR Speak to Rock?

I have heard that drugs will be the great equalizer when the tough times hits the West. The so called war on drugs has been an abysmal failure in the United States, and other Western countries. Although you may not see crack heads roaming your beautiful suburban neighborhood, the abuse of prescription drugs behind closed doors is just as prevalent. In the event of major war breaking out or a solar storm shutting down the electrical grid, some people will turn into absolute animals without their drug of choice.

Years ago, I was restoring an abandoned crack house in the Liberty City section of Miami, Florida. My relatives purchased the four unit property from the city for pennies on the dollar. Since I was fresh out of college and not paying rent, my mother figured I should be helping with the repairs on the property for free. The wiring in the apartments was still good but we had to remove some of the walls, add new blocks, plaster, etc. We had to purchase a few tons of concrete and gravel to bring the place up to code. Since we didn't budget for the proper construction equipment, my mom realized we were under manned for this job. She decided to hire the local crack heads to help us with the hauling of the gravel and concrete around the construction site. We paid two crack heads $10 each to help move the tons of construction debris onto the site and into the dump truck. Our jaws dropped to the floor in amazement as these frail and skinny men lugged these hundred pound blocks around like paper weights. They moved 300lb machinery up a flight of stairs like a mother carrying a bag of groceries. The other workers including myself stopped at this display of super human strength.

I noticed my Uncle Howard (a former drug addict) sitting down under a palm tree, sipping iced tea and laughing hysterically. I asked him, "What is so funny? Aren't you scared these skinny dudes may get hurt?"

Uncle Howard replies, "They will be just fine. These jokers are in a rush to get their next hit, and nothing will stop them." His words would remain with me forever.

Sure enough, the two drug addicts completed their assigned tasks with no injury. Even though they were about 5 foot 8 and 120 pounds soaking wet, they did the work of 6 men in a little under an hour. As soon as they received their money they quickly left to get their "medicine". (The word "medicine" is used to identify both legal and illegal substances in Miami.)

We hear stories of six police officers restraining one man high on drugs yet we quickly forget those stories until we are confronted with such a person. The media would have us believe that only people abusing uncontrolled substances act in such a manner, but I say prescription drugs are just as dangerous when abused. The rash of school shootings throughout the United States were primarily committed by people on psychotropic drugs. A fact that our controlled media chooses to conveniently ignore.

So what's the point you ask? The people in society that have uncontrollable drug addictions pose a danger to themselves as well as their fellow citizens in a grid down situation. If Manny the meth head can not get his methamphetamines in a timely manner, Manny may lose it. If Zack does not get his Zoloft, chances are Zack could get zany. Are you a prepper that has trouble kicking a drug habit? What if your prepper neighbor's kid is strung out? What if there is suspected drug house in your bug out location?

The Solution is Prayer

Have you ever tried praying over the situation or the person? I have noticed that many people have been able to kick drug habits by people laying hands and praying over them. In some cases the deliverance is immediate albeit other cases the prayer will have to be mixed with fasting. Substance abuse issues are sometimes demons that have embedded themselves onto the person through their particular vice. The one thing a demon truly fears is a Christian that really knows how to apply the word of God. It's a sad reality when I can watch one of those exorcism television shows and the non-Christian actually knows how to apply bible verses better than people who have been attending a church for twenty years. It is best to know how to apply God's word rather than just be a pew sitter. If you are serious about prepping for the future, knowing how to apply God's word to your daily life could be a life saver.

Let me tell you the story of my friend Alvin the handyman. Alvin was known throughout Miami as the best handyman to never show up to work. If he showed up to a job, he could fix just about anything he put his hands on. He was skilled in all facets of home repair and his prices were cheap. The only problem with Alvin was that he was unreliable due to his alcohol abuse. It was common to find Alvin working on your house with a bottle of Jamaican Wray & Nephew 80 proof rum next to his lunch box. The bottle should have been attached to his tool belt because they both were used during the work day. The problem was never Alvin's quality of work, the problem was getting him to show up for work. Due to his drinking issues, he would over sleep do to hangovers. One day he was doing work for my mother's house and he began to miss days because of his drinking. My mother complained about the situation to a Christian evangelist named Pastor Cecile Fisher or Sister Fisher as she is affectionately known. Sister Fisher decided to come talk to Alvin the next time he showed up to work. With her piercing brown eyes and heavy Jamaican accent, she told Mr. Alvin that God loves him and has a plan for his life. Mister Alvin thought Sister Fisher was nuts but she persisted in talking to him while he was working. Eventually he relented and said "if God could take this desire to drink booze from me, I will serve him." Sister Fisher asked him to pray with her and Alvin accepted her request. Since I was a teenager at the time, I do not remember the whole prayer nor all the words that came from Sister Fisher's mouth but this one of those moments that remains etched in my memory. During the prayer Sister Fisher said, "In the name of Jesus, I curse every demon of alcohol off this body and this body will now treat alcohol as poison."

I didn't understand the power of that prayer until I seen Mr. Alvin a few weeks later at a mutual friends house in Miami. The same handyman that always carried his trademark Wray & Nephew brand bottle of rum was visibly sober. Alvin's nappy hair was combed and he was neatly shaved. The clothing he was wearing actually smelled like fabric softener instead of cigarettes from the local bar and get this; drum roll please; he had a bible in his hand!

Do you recall what Jesus did to the fig tree and the result? In the book of Mark (11:12-25), it is recorded that Jesus cursed a fig tree for not bearing any fruit when he came by. When he and his disciples came walking by later, the disciples found the tree withered to death from the roots up. In the book of Proverbs (18:21) it says, "Death and life are in the power of the tongue: and they that love it shall eat the fruit thereof." Sister Fisher knew these principles that is why she used them to help Alvin beat his addiction. She also knew that if Alvin accepted Jesus as his savior, God will supernaturally help him kick the bottle. Sister Fisher knew by speaking life over Alvin, he could be set free and she also knew that if she cursed the demon of alcohol, the roots of this demon would wither and die.

As preppers, we must use caution when speaking harmful words over another human being. If there is a friend in your preparedness group that is struggling with an addiction, maybe you and your friends should begin praying over that person when you have meetings. Do it as many times as it takes and as long as that person is honest about their particular addiction and as long as they are not committing any crimes to support their habit. Just be careful not to enable a drug addict's behavior!

I know of a family of preppers that has a son that abuses illegal drugs. Every time the young man would get into trouble, the family would bail him out of jail. They reasoned to themselves that he just needed more rehab classes. He would go to classes to please his parents, but not to get free from his addictions. The young man would continue his crimes to support his drug binges and his parents would continually bail him out of jail. If I were the parent, I would let him stay in jail to learn a lesson. There comes a point when you can become as guilty as the criminal, if you enable their behavior. This young man became a danger to a prepping community because of his stealing and his parent's lack of discipline.

Speak to the Crack Cocaine Rock?

In the book of Numbers, we find Moses in the desert with the children of Israel. Naturally people get thirsty when they are in a desert so they began to demand water from Moses. Moses asks God for help and God tells Moses to go to certain rocky area and then "speak to the rock and it will give the people water." Rather than being obedient to what God tells him, Moses goes to the rock and beats it with his rod in anger. The end result was Moses being sentenced to exile in the wilderness for his disobedience. (Numbers 20:5-12)

How many times have we been tempted to smash the rock rather than just speak to it? Too often. One day at a gun show in Hickory, North Carolina an ammunition dealer was visibly angry. Most people were avoiding him but I went up and asked what's wrong? He explained that the local police have not done anything with the illicit drug house in his neighborhood even though he has given the police videotaped evidence. His wife and kids were now scared to walk in their own neighborhood, especially because the drug addicts would use their backyard as a shortcut to get to the drug den. The neighbors would no longer let their children play in the streets for fear of them being harmed. He explained to me that house is as busy as a fast food drive thru because of the amount of traffic coming to the house twenty four hours a day. He confided in me and told me that if the police do not go over their make some arrests, he would go over there in the middle of the night with his AR-15 and clean house. Sensing the seriousness of this gentleman I would not name for security reasons, I told him about an easier way to deal with the situation since the police wouldn't. He told me to let him know because he has tried everything. I noticed that this young man was just like Moses in the wilderness.

I asked him, "Are you a Christian?"

He replies, "Absolutely."

I said, "That's good to hear, because Jesus wouldn't want you to run into the drug house with your guns blazing. Just pray with me over this crack house and believe God for a miracle."

The ammunition dealer says, "It sounds so simple but hey, I am willing to try anything right now."

I laid a hand on his shoulder and prayed right in the middle of the gun show. Faith does not care about who is looking and neither should you. Interesting enough, another Christian came by and laid hands on my shoulder and joined us in prayer asking God to close down the crack house. Three months later I saw the ammo dealer and his smile went from one end of the room to the other. He yelled out, "The crack house is empty and they are gone!"

This man was about to do the same thing Moses did in the wilderness: use brute force when the only thing required was speaking to the situation. Had he went into the drug house and shot a few of the drug abusers he may have made the situation worse than before. The reality is that all he had to do was speak life rather than bring death.

To the prepper reading this in the future: The situation you are facing may not be as bad as you think. Is there a less brutal way of solving the problem? As preppers we have to constantly remind ourselves that guns and knives are for self defense. Prayer is a form of speaking to the rocks and boulders in your life. Jesus said it best:

And Jesus said unto them, Because of your unbelief: for verily I say unto you, If ye have faith as a grain of mustard seed, ye shall say unto this mountain, Remove hence to yonder place; and it shall remove; and nothing shall be impossible unto you.
Matthew 17:20

During one of my recent trips to England I encountered a retired British special forces operative having drinks outside a pub with his friend. I met them outside of a pub with his drinking partner. They heard my American accent and invited me over to have a beer. I declined the beer but I did sit and chat with them for over an hour. We talked about politics and sports, but the Holy Spirit told me that I must tell the veteran about Jesus. Easier said than done because this dude had enough scars and tattoos to make any Hollywood makeup artist blush. I can tell he has had his share of bar brawls and legal problems since leaving the military. Somehow the subject of religion came up and the retired military man claimed he was an atheist. I simply told him, "Jesus believes in you." The demons in this tattooed dude hated that statement because he got irate. He told me, "Your f—king Jesus doesn't bloody exist!" Now I had three choices at this moment:

1) I could wimp out and deny my convictions.
2) I could throw the first punch because he was ready to fight.
3) I could speak to the rock.

I chose to speak to the rock. Since Christ is my rock, I quickly said under my breath, "Lord Jesus help me". Jesus is the rock of a true believer's life, so you must learn to lean on him in dangerous situations. I still didn't know if his friend would pounce on me either, so I knew it would be okay to seek heavenly backup. (So much for a friendly chat outside the pub.) The other rock I had to speak with was this hardened military veteran.

I then said, "Deep in your heart, you don't believe that man. You know Jesus loves you."

He then became angrier and said, "Loves who? Can you see the darkness in my heart? You and your Jesus s--- is just bloody nonsense!"

I said in a louder voice, "Jesus loves you!"

He grew angrier and yelled insults and a couple of colorful cuss words.

I then raised my voice and said, "I bind the lying demon off you! Jesus loves you!"

At this moment we were face to face and the Holy Spirit took full control. He hurled more insults with a bit of spit landing in my face, I yelled, "Jesus loves you" for every insult.

Eventually, I noticed the demon that controlled him became weaker every time I yelled, "Jesus loves you!" I knew he was ready to punch me in the nose but something was forcing him to hear me tell him those same words.

Then a crack in the armor appeared. He yelled in my face, "If your bloody Jesus loves me so much, I want him to show up in my damn bedroom and tell me so himself!"

I yelled, "Fine. He will. Take my hand and let's pray!" I grabbed his hand like a pro wrestler and he angrily grabbed mine back. I closed my eyes and prayed aloud that God would take all the anger out of his heart and for Jesus to fill his heart with love, and furthermore for Jesus to visit him in his room at night to tell him how much He loves him."

I turned my head for a punch to the side of my face and instead something miraculous happened. The hardened military veteran gave me a hug and cried on my arm like a baby. Jesus Christ had visited a pub that day in England.

For the future, preppers must know that violence doesn't solve anything. The bible says, "If it be possible, live peaceably with all men." (Rom 12:18) If you are prepping, your best prep is to have Jesus Christ in your heart. With Christ inside of you, I know you will be the best equipped to handle differences with people you do not get along with. Sometimes, it's better to just speak to the rock.

Chapter 6

When there is no doctor...

There is a popular book among folks in the preparedness community called "When there is no doctor". It gives readers some great first aid advice for the numerous types of situations they may encounter when modern emergency services are unavailable. I think every house in the Western World should have a copy of it sitting in their home right next to the bible.

There is common misconception among the majority of the people in the United States, Canada, and Great Britain. The misconception is that emergency services will always be there to rescue you from misfortune. The people are programmed to believe that once they call 911 or the like, they will have immediate access to medical services should the need arise. Whether it becomes a slip and fall accident or a heart attack, the populace can expect an ambulance with a skilled doctor on the way.

This is where the preppers of the world differ from the population. We take notice of the different situations around the world when emergency services were abruptly cut off. The prepper community took careful notice of the devastation caused by the Asian Tsunami in 2004 and Hurricane Katrina's wake of destruction in 2005. Perhaps your attention was captured during the life shattering Haitian earthquake of 2010 or the constant civil wars in today's Middle Eastern countries. The prepper community noticed the one thing the masses did not: There were no emergency services for weeks and sometimes months.

During these situations people will naturally call the emergency services for medical help. The question is: What do people do when there is no help coming? Like all these situations I mentioned, there wasn't any immediate help coming for days,

weeks or months. A good example is the testimony of Selco. This gentleman lived in Bosnia when war broke out in 1992. He carefully explains on his online blogs the speed in which a normal civilized society will decend into chaos. People were forced to realize that emergency services are null and void. His testimonies are free to read on the internet at:
http://shtfschool.com/general/signs-of-shtf/

I respect the fact that many people in the emergency preparedness community are learning basic life saving skills like CPR, sutures and so forth. This is invaluable information during an emergency scenario. During the many classes I have attended at preparedness meetings, I noticed people lack the spiritual edge needed to overcome these medical emergencies. Let's be real, we all do not have a registered nurse or a general practitioner of medicine in our family. Many of our friends in the preparedness community need to be real about their strengths and their weaknesses. We are all not skilled in medicine or the treatment of ailments. My purpose for this chapter is to help you tap into the healing power that God has given you, so that you may utilize these abilities to save lives in the future, and perhaps even your own.

When there is no money, there is no doctor!

People in the United States are growing quite aware of our countries dreadful financial situation. Many financial analysts say another Great Depression is an absolute certainty. If this is indeed the case, then we should expect the same lack of medical services especially if the common man will not be able to pay for it.

My good friend Russel in North Carolina is an example. Growing up during the Great Depression, Russel was one of the many children that contracted the dreaded Scarlett Fever. This infectious disease which commonly affected children was a dreaded killer during the years of the depression. Russel's parents did not have any financial means of caring for their sick son. Ten year old Russel looked like he would suffer the same fate as every other child that contracted the disease because his 100 pound body slowly deteriorated to 35 pounds. Even though the neighbors had written Russel off for dead, his mother and grandmother literally prayed over the boy every day and night. Miraculously, Russel had a full recovery with no medical intervention. The point is we may be forced to do exactly what the bible says to do in these situations in the future.

Is any sick among you? let him call for the elders of the church; and let them pray over him, anointing him with oil in the name of the Lord:
James 5:14

Mount of Transfiguration

My good friend Pastor Charlie Reed was on a hiking trip in a remote part of the Appalachian Mountains with some young hikers. At one point, the elder Charlie injured his foot and was practically unable to walk. His fellow hikers became extremely nervous because they were miles out of cell phone range and the decent down the mountain was treacherous to say the least. Charlie assured everyone he would be fine because God wanted him to preach at a church that evening. The young hikers present looked at him like he was going delirious from the pain. Charlie's ankle and foot had become a dark shade of purple. The swelling was so severe that Charlie could no longer wear his hiking boot. The hikers begged Charlie to let them hike down mountain to call an emergency helicopter to bring him to the hospital. Now had this been a person that does not conduct spiritual workouts, this offer would indeed seem logical. However, Charlie is rare breed of Christian; in evangelical circles they refer to him as a "prayer warrior". These are Christians that make praying and fasting a normal routine as one would brush their teeth in the morning. Charlie calmly prayed to God to heal him so he could get down the mountain to preach at the church that night. The hikers reluctantly made a set of makeshift crutches for Charlie. He told them to walk ahead and that he would catch up with them. As Charlie took each step the pain became unbearable, but he prayed with every step he took. After about one hundred yards, he felt a splash of water around his swollen lower leg. He looked to see if he had stepped unwittingly into a puddle only to see dry ground. Curious, he rolled up his jeans and pulled off the wet sock that was covering the injured ankle and foot. To Charlie's surprise, the entire ankle and foot returned to normal color. The elephant sized foot swelling was totally gone! Charlie got up and walked pain free down the mountain. He eventually caught up to the younger hikers and even beat some of them back to their destination.

Extreme Medical Training

As a prepper, I encourage people to learn medical basics like CPR, and treatment of cuts and sprains. Have an ample supply of vitamins, medicines, and bandages. God gave man the wisdom to create these things to treat our bodies for the minor mishaps with our health.

I don't mind some preppers learning the advanced treatments, but I always advise you to use caution with what you're taking. Just because someone says it works does not mean it works. People tend to operate from rumor rather than fact or even experience for that matter. A fellow prepper once told me that bentonite clay is great to use for emergency snake bite treatment. One day my best friend was bitten by a snake on the foot and we administered bentonite clay around the foot, upper ankle and calf. We waited hours but the condition worsened. Then it dawned on me, that I only took the report of one person regarding bentonite clay and snake bites. After I did my own research online, I found that it is a good natural health product for removing certain impurities, toxins, and metals from the body, but it did not remove snake venom in our experience. I found testimonies of it being used after spider bites and perhaps those reports are true considering a spider bite does not go as deep as snake fangs. Experience is much more valuable to me than just talk. Try to find real life testimonials regarding alternative treatments and products. You do not want to be in a grid down situation to find out the amazing health product you have in your bug out bag is an amazing waste of money.

One particular preparedness group I know of in North Carolina puts experience to the forefront of their medical teaching. For example, the instructor of the class would teach you how to treat a wound on a piece of meat from the butcher shop. He would show you what to look for in determining the cause of the wound such as a knife or a bullet. He would then show you how to extract the bullet if necessary and the proper application of sutures / stitches.

The very next day in the outdoor class he would announce a pop quiz. The students would pull out pens and paper awaiting his questions. Since it was an out door class under a tent, he would have an assistant walk a large pig over from a truck. The instructor would quickly pull out a gun and shoot the pig. Bang! He would them yell at his students to perform immediate surgery. Some of the students would do an excellent job meanwhile other students would faint from trauma. I've heard that every pig he has used has survived the class! Animal rights groups would love to hammer this guy but I do understand his unruly methods. He understands that experience is the best teacher in real life situations. Some preppers think they can administer medical aid to a friend with a gun shot wound is like giving band aids to a child's scraped knee. They have to realize that their will be screams and lots of warm blood. The medical books in the library can not teach the hands on experience.

This is why this book you are reading tells of all the different experiences people have endured in crisis situations. Without God, these people including myself, would have failed miserably. I noticed that when Christians have an experience of God supernaturally moving in crisis situations, the Bible itself is no longer just a book and their life becomes a living testimony. The same applies to the prepper. The more experience the prepper may have will exponentially help them in a crisis. Now if we can learn to take our best experiences from the natural realm and combine it with our best supernatural experiences, the possibilities of survival become endless.

Sticky Fingers

Speaking of not going to the doctor, Aliss Cresswell out of England told an interesting story on the television show **Its Supernatural**. Aliss told the story of reformed criminal having pains in is hands. It turns out ten years earlier shattered window glass entered his hands during a burglary. He could not go to the doctor for fear of being discovered by the police for his criminal misconduct. So he chose to let his hands suffer the pain instead of medical intervention. The hands never fully healed and he was stricken with constant pain. Upon hearing the story at her café, she asked them man to give her hands so she can pray over them. He agreed to the prayer and simply put his hands in her hands. Aliss prayed the following words, "In Jesus name, I command all the glass to be removed from this body and to be healed." The former burglar came back to her shop the next day and reported that tiny shards of glass had been supernaturally coming out of his finger tips all night. He was moving his hands normally and no longer in any pain!

Blanks or Bullets?

Well, if God can do that for shards of glass, can he do it for a bullet? I believe he can. One day I met a Christian missionary at a preparedness show in North Carolina. He told me he recently went on dangerous missionary trip to Pakistan and has seen some of the most mind boggling events to take place. One particular day some armed radical Islamic gunmen came to their outdoor church crusade with loaded AK-47 rifles. The men fired the guns in the air thus frightening hundreds of Pakistani Christians to run for their lives. The gunmen then walked to the Pastors by the podium and demanded they tell everyone remaining to leave or they will be killed. One of the Pastor's response to the gunmen was simply a brazen act of faith or stupidity, because he said, "we will not leave because our God will protect us." The masked gunmen then fired a few shots in the air and then repeated their demand. This time, the other pastors present joined the first pastor in responding by saying, "We will not leave, our God will protect us." The gunmen then pointed the AK-47 rifles at the men and pressed the triggers. Miraculously, every one of the rifles had a bullet jam. The men checked the guns, cleared the jammed bullet and pulled the triggers again. The guns did not fire nor did they jam. This time the triggers on their rifles became stuck. The men were confused because the guns were in proper working order moments earlier. Then one of the men aimed his rifle to the sky and pulled the trigger. Bang! The gun worked just fine. The other men did the same action by pointing their gun in the air and pulling the trigger. All of their guns worked like normal. They pointed the guns at the Pastors again and tried to shoot their rifles. Every rifle trigger froze again! Frustrated the men kept trying to pull the trigger and nothing would happen. In their frustration they began to argue with each other and complaining about the frozen triggers on the guns. As they argued and pointed the guns at each other, the guns then went off. The men accidently shot each other! Contrary to popular belief, an extremist isn't exactly welcomed at every hospital in Pakistan. In some areas, an educated Pakistani views them as a nuisance to the community. So, unless they had an extremist doctor nearby, they had slim chances of receiving good medical treatment. In an act of mercy, the Pastors surrounded the gunmen and laid hands upon their wounds and prayed over the men. People watched in amazement as the gaping bullet wounds miraculously closed and the gunmen were healed. The gunmen immediately accepted Jesus Christ as their Lord and Master. To this very day, these men are now employed as armed bodyguards for Christians visiting Pakistan!

Steps of Faith

People ask me all the time, "Brother Keith, why are these amazing miracles happening in third world countries and not America?" My answer to the question is simple: Those brothers and sisters exercise their faith. They are conditioned to rely on God for everything in those places meanwhile people in the Western World rely on technology. Many of the third world countries do not have the luxury of modern medicine nearby so they have to trust God with an absolute certainty. Now don't misunderstand my views on seeking medical attention when necessary. If you have a serious medical emergency, by all means, seek medical help. God has also blessed the earth with good doctors and medicine. However, there will be some situations in the Western World especially in the United States, when there will be no earthly doctor available whether it be from natural disaster, civil unrest, or war. Each person reading this book will make the critical choice of relying on God's word or to give up hope and die. I choose to live my life by faith and by faith in the word of God.

Since my faith is in God and not in medicine, perhaps my next statement will not shock you. Many preppers are concerned about the availability of certain medicines before God renders his judgments on America. (Oh, yes I did say God will judge America.)Yes, it is wise to store up on the medicines you take, so put some aside. But, what if the crisis time exceeds the amount of medicine you have? The honest truth is the prepper without faith will die, and the prepper with faith will live. The bible clearly says, "...faith without works is dead."(James 2:26)

My advice to the prepper that requires constant medicine is to begin praying fervently to God for a healing over your body. Don't accept the fact that your medical condition is permanent. The God that created heaven and earth is smart enough to cure your tiny body. Start annoying God like a child would annoy a parent for their toy. Eventually, God gets annoyed with your nagging Him and decides to give in. Jesus Christ gave us an illustration when he spoke this parable:

2Saying, There was in a city a judge, which feared not God, neither regarded man:
3And there was a widow in that city; and she came unto him, saying, Avenge me of mine adversary.
4And he would not for a while: but afterward he said within himself, Though I fear not God, nor regard man;
5Yet because this widow troubleth me, I will avenge her, lest by her continual coming she weary me.
6And the Lord said, Hear what the unjust judge saith.
7And shall not God avenge his own elect, which cry day and night unto him, though he bear long with them?
(Luke 18:2-7)

Another key to allowing God to supernaturally heal your body is to forgive people. If you are holding any unforgiveness or grudges towards any human being, I highly advise that you forgive the person. Unforgiveness in your heart towards another human being actually blocks your physical and emotional healings. I have seen people come off of chemotherapy treatments and supernaturally get healed from stage four cancer simply because they chose to forgive all the people that hurt them.

But if ye forgive not men their trespasses, neither will your Father forgive your trespasses. (Matthew 6:15)

Get radical

Jesus was a radical dude. If you have ever read the gospels concerning Jesus, he didn't exactly try to fit in. He stood out and so did his faith. But you know something? He loves when you let your faith in Him stand out. If you are a prepper with a serious ailment, just how far would you go to prove to God that you believe in his divine healing? I suggest you let God see some action behind your words. A friend of mine named Jerry from Florida proved the point I am trying to make to you. Jerry is a prepper just like you and me. Like many preppers in the United States, Jerry fears an economic collapse is imminent. So he has taken steps to ensure his families safety in the event the U.S. dollar becomes worthless. After years of careful money management, Jerry was shocked when the doctor told him that he had cancer. A cancerous mole was rapidly growing on Jerry's face and the doctor told Jerry that he would need chemotherapy. Jerry tells the doctor that he just needs "Jesus". As far as Jerry was concerned, having chemo treatments would not bode well for him during a societal collapse. Jerry decided it was time to stretch his faith. He started reading his bible more often and combined it with constant prayer. Then he did something rather odd. Every morning and night he would look in the mirror at the tumor on his face, lay his hand over it and pray for God to heal him. Jerry repeated this process for countless days. One evening Jerry took the radical behavior a step further. He decided to reenact what Jesus did to the fig tree in the book of Mark chapter 11. Jerry laid his hand over the tumor and prayed these words out loud, "Cancer, I curse you in Jesus name! Leave my body!" At that moment the ungodly mole on his face burst into water. Jerry removed the dead skin and the spot where the tumor was appeared like a newborn's skin. To this very day, Jerry is cancer free!

Now is the time to begin exercising your faith! Do not wait until the tough times come to attempt to jump start your faith. Faith is like a muscle. It needs to be stretched and pulled like a weight lifter in the gym. After working it out in numerous situations, it gets stronger and stronger. In order to survive the tsunami of tribulations coming to the United States, I realized that my faith in God must be at an optimal level at all times. Can we raise your faith? I believe so...

And Jesus said unto them, Because of your unbelief: for verily I say unto you, If ye have faith as a grain of mustard seed, ye shall say unto this mountain, Remove hence to yonder place; and it shall remove; and nothing shall be impossible unto you.
(Matthew 17:20)

Chapter 7

Physical Fitness or Spiritual Fitness?

Are you the type of reader that enjoys a leisurely jog around the neighborhood? Perhaps you are the type that does not miss a day at the gym with your personal trainer? Or maybe a workout to you means looking around the house for the remote control? Either way, people in our western society look at physical fitness in different ways. I know some folks that work on their farm all day doing hard manual labor and there are others that run around an office getting the business reports to the boss. The truth of the matter is that many of us in Western society tend to mistake being busy with physical fitness. A man that works at a computer desk all day can be extremely busy and have a mentally draining day but it does not make him physically fit.

If you are person that is into a prepping lifestyle but you are lacking physical fitness, may I kindly advise you that you can not have one without the other. During the dreadful day of 9/11 many New Yorkers found themselves stranded in lower Manhattan with no transportation home. All of the public transportation for the borough of Manhattan were immediately suspended. People were forced to walk for miles to get home. Speaking at a press conference at 11:02am on the morning of the attacks, Mayor Giuliani told New Yorkers: "If you are south of Canal Street, get out. Walk slowly and carefully. If you can't figure what else to do, just walk north."

This quote came directly from:
U.S. Department of Transportation, Research and Special Programs Administration, Volpe National Transportation Systems Center (April 2002). "EFFECTS OF CATASTROPHIC EVENTS ON

TRANSPORTATION SYSTEM MANAGEMENT AND OPERATIONS: NEW YORK CITY- SEPTEMBER 11"

I found this quote troubling on many different levels. This was when I began to see the need to be physically prepared for disasters and emergencies. People in western society always believe that an ambulance or police man will be there for the catastrophes we may encounter. Your greatest asset in the physical realm will not be your guns, but It will actually be your overall health. You may be forced to walk for miles to get to safety. Many of my personal friends that endured that tragic day in New York told me they had to walk from lower Manhattan to Yonkers. For those of you that do not know the distance, lets just say twenty miles. They could not get the usual subway train to take them north, buses were suspended, and cabs were near non existent. Good Samaritans found it difficult to give someone a ride with their vehicle because of road blocks or traffic jams. We hear of the people killed in the World Trade Centers and the Pentagon attacks but what about the victims of collateral damage. Many people died from heart conditions meanwhile others were hospitalized for other serious ailments resulting from their attempted journey home.

I have noticed some folks in the emergency preparedness community are in the worst physical shape. Sure they may have plenty of money to buy preparedness items like long term food and gold, but their physical health is oft ignored. Start asking your self this question: If an emergency occurred, will I be able to walk 10 miles to safety? What about 20 miles? What about doing this type of walk through the forest? These are questions that people need to ask themselves if they plan on "bugging out" on foot.

At the time of writing this chapter, I just worked a gun show in Greenville, South Carolina. There was an out of shape gentleman purchasing items at my booth for his preparations for financial collapse. He believed in having some extra food provisions stored away as well as physical gold and silver to help his family in the event the U.S. dollar loses its purchasing power. I asked him the same question I ask all of my customers, "Do you have a relationship with God." He then proudly tells me that he is an atheist. Now obviously I would like to share the gospel of Jesus Christ with this man, but he said he has heard it before and blah, blah, blah. Since I do not believe in forcing anyone to share my beliefs on God, I figured I would just pray for him. But here is the kicker: I noticed that his physical preparation was just as lacking as his spiritual preparation. Since I have met him on few occasions, I have taken notice of his need to lose weight as well as his ability to lose his temper. If this particular gentleman were put into a situation where he needed to hike 20 miles to get to safety, I would say the chances of him making it would be slim, I would also say that he is at a greater disadvantage because of his lack of belief in God. Now don't get me wrong, there are some people that are well proportioned and still maintain a high level of physical fitness. A friend of mine from Syracuse named Shawan was one of those guys. He looked big and fat but he was one of the most athletically gifted people I knew. So there are exceptions to the rule. But people need to be honest with themselves, especially when it comes to surviving disaster scenarios. The scene in the movies where the inexperienced office manager gets lost while on his first camping trip and hikes twenty miles through the mountains is a fantasy unless there is a supernatural element.

    This is where spiritual fitness comes in to break the barriers of what is deemed possible. One of the most powerful things Jesus Christ has ever said is "All things are possible to him that believes." As a pastor, preparedness expert, and motivational speaker, I understand fully that our beliefs will set the bar on where we can go in life and on our spiritual walk. I believe that Jesus Christ actually means what he says in the scriptures and his words are more reliable than any check being deposited in your bank account. I believe wholeheartedly the warnings he gave in Matthew chapter 24 were for 2000 years ago as well as today. With that being said, I also believe that if preppers can be less carnal and more spiritual, they will actually handle any disaster situation much better. It will start by not only being a follower of Jesus Christ, but be willing to exercise your spiritual muscles. Three of your foundational spiritual exercises will be prayer, fasting and reading the bible.

Reading the bible may seem old fashioned to some people, but every building needs a foundation. Ask many professional athletes about their training regimens and they will say the foundational exercises are the most important. For example, most people assume professional boxers focus training sessions on their punching power when the reality is the foundation of their training is on their legs. Why? It's their leg strength that actually aids their punches. It is their leg balance and quick feet that helps them avoid hits. It's their strong legs that help them stand with an opponent during a grueling 15 round match. To sum it up properly: If a boxer does not train his legs, his chances of winning are very slim. Many of the so-called foundational secrets I use to heal people of diseases, deliver them from suicidal thoughts, and to pay my bills were found in the bible. It wasn't a secret at all. Its a willingness to let God use you and to believe His words written in the bible. In addition to belief, I was willing to read through the bible on multiple occasions. Through that discipline, I noticed these words began to aid me in my life. When I found myself urinating blood one day, I immediately began quoting healing verses out of the bible out loud. Realizing it must be kidney related, I asked my wife to lay hands over my kidneys and pray over them since it is healing practice found in the bible. (She used other healing verses from the bible during her prayer I might add.) The end result was that I was healed and I didn't require any medication or surgery! My question to you is: will you let God build a foundation upon you? I say this because one day you may be a building block in your community after a disaster. A strong community will need to be built on a strong foundation before someone decides its better to rebuild on sand.

If the foundations be destroyed, what can the righteous do? (Psalm 11:3)

Olympic Strength without going to the Gym

Many people are familiar with the biblical story of Samson and Delilah. People pose questions regarding Samson's super human strength. Was it just his long hair that enabled him to have such strength or was it his relationship with God? I choose not to answer the question because I thought it was more pertinent to investigate biblical history for other cases of super human strength. The results were fascinating! By carefully examining both biblical and extra-biblical sources I found out that high levels of spiritual fitness can manifest itself into physical fitness. One man to highlight is the prophet Elijah. Arguably, one of the most famous prophets in the bible, this man performed many miracles including raising the dead. Elijah the prophet was known to pray and fast. His prayers became a terror to his enemies because he even prayed for it not to rain, and it brought the kingdom to financial ruin by means of a three and half year drought. However, when he prayed for the rain to return the bible says:

45And it came to pass in the mean while, that the heaven was black with clouds and wind, and there was a great rain. And Ahab rode, and went to Jezreel.
46And the hand of the LORD was on Elijah; and he girded up his loins, and ran before Ahab to the entrance of Jezreel.
(1 Kings 45:46)

Think about this for a second. There was a severe famine because of the drought. Food was scarce due to the water shortage. Through clear circumstantial evidence we know that Elijah was an old man yet he was able to out run Ahab's chariot by the distance of 17 miles? (The distance from Mount Carmel to Jezreel)

Hey, I am a big fan of the Jamaican Track and Field team, especially with their track star Usain Bolt. I love to watch him leave his opponents in the dust during the 100 and 200 yard dash. Yet, to see a bald headed old man like Elijah run with that speed over rocky terrain and sand for miles is a showdown of the spiritual realm invading the physical realm.

The thin line between Dreams & Reality

There has been medical studies taken while a person is sleeping that shows the raise in heart beats per minute and increased breathing. Many of the subjects dreamed of running or some other strenuous activity. Even though they were dreaming, there physical body believed the reality of their dream. When your spiritual fitness is strong, it begins to manifest itself in your physical reality.

During numerous periods in my life I would abstain from eating any foods to enhance my spiritual strength. To the Christians, Muslims and Jews this practice is known as fasting. I can say with all humility, I have secretly done this by surviving on only fluids. I did not say smoothies, I said fluids. During this time I prayed more and read the bible more often.

I can painfully recall the 19th day of fasting with no food. I seriously felt like I was going to die. I prayed earnestly to God for help to complete the fast. That night I went to sleep and the coolest thing happened. I dreamt I was in a supermarket with the best looking food you can imagine. Every food on the planet was available; from filet mignon to strawberry cheesecake. The people in the supermarket were all extremely polite and they were sharing the different gourmet foods with each other. The store manager calls me over to him and asks me to come into his office. We sit in his office which had the appearance of a VIP room for travelers at the airport. I looked out his office windows and noticed we were in the clouds. The view outside his office window was breath taking. As we sat down and had a chat, the man congratulated me for "making it this far". He told me, "God is very pleased with your obedience."

After a few minutes of chatting, he pulled out a plastic Ziploc bag with some type of white colored trail mix. He ate some of it and offered me some. I asked him, "What is it?" He simply replied, "Just trust me kid, your going to like it." I was so weak in the dream, I could barely raise my hand to get the first scoop in my mouth, so he put some on his hand and fed it to me. As I chewed the food, I felt my energy returning to my body. Then I felt strong enough to begin eating the food with my own hand. The food looked like finely grounded coconut with yellow coriander seeds scattered inside it. However it tasted like honey and granola with a tiny pinch of salt. The man in the dream told me to have the rest. I asked him, "Are you sure?' He replied, "Yes, consider it a gift." The next morning I woke up in my bed but I still tasted the actual food on my tongue. Freaked out, I began checking my pillow for crumbs but I could not find any. I told my wife and she said, "Honey, I think you were given manna!"

(Manna was the food that rained from the sky on the children of Israel to feed them during their stay in the desert in the book of Exodus chapter 16. It is also referred to as "Angels food" in the book of Psalms 78:25.)

Miraculously, I felt like a new man. I could have run five miles with the high school track team if you asked me to. I immediately put on my clothes and went to work. Up until that point I had stopped working my landscaping job because I was too weak, but this time I was operating the heavy machinery at work with confidence. It was a supernatural high I can never fully explain. I was no longer hungry for food!

If a serious disaster or emergency happened in your neck of the woods tomorrow, and food was no longer available, can your spiritual fitness over compensate for your physical fitness? Yes, it can. My hope is that the average semi spiritual prepper out there in the reading audience will take some of the gems I am giving and turn them into a jewelry store. I am not a better human being than you because the reality is that I am your servant. My calling is to help equip my brothers and sisters in the preparedness community with the unobstructed gifts of the Holy Spirit. It is these spiritual gifts that will make the under average prepper into the above average prepper. The deadly realities we face in the future will be much easier to face when your spiritually strong. If you read your bible and cross check some of things I am speaking about, perhaps you will learn these principles to strengthen your inner spirit man.

Two Nephews

My church will occasionally conduct a healing meeting every few months. I will normally pray and fast for a few days before the actual meeting to increase my spiritual strength. On the day of the meeting, I had to work a gun show in Greenville, South Carolina. I was pretty upset that I could not physically attend the meeting because of work but I still decided to fast from food. I remember telling friends at church that the meeting will come with me to South Carolina. While at the gun show, a friend of mine informed me that his two nephews were both in the hospital dying of stage 4 cancer. The men were both in their early twenties and it seemed like a tragic ending in the making because the treatments were not working. My friend asked me to come by and pray for them and I accepted. I simply laid hands on them, prayed and rebuked the cancer in Jesus name. Three months later I seen my friend from Greenville and he ran and hugged me. He told me that both of his nephews are back at work and the cancer is gone from their bodies!

And he stood over her, and rebuked the fever; and it left her: and immediately she arose and ministered unto them. (Luke 4:39)

There are fast approaching days when we will not have the luxury of a clean hospital with board certified doctors to treat our ailments. If we won't have access to the expensive medical treatments , we must be strong enough spiritually to look death in the eye and tell it to leave. Start learning to prep on the spiritual side!

Holding it together

Please do not misunderstand my views on physical fitness. I think it is wise to keep your physical body in the best shape possible. However, when the tough times come, it isn't always your physical prowess to give you the advantage. Your spiritual strength can take you places your physical body can not take you. In an emergency situation, your spiritual preps will take you much farther than you think.

My spiritual brother Emmanuel Twagirimana from Rwanda is a living testimony of spiritual strength in the jaws of death. Although he stands only five foot eight inches tall, the inner strength God has given this man is remarkable. Emmanuel was one of the many people that barely survived the civil war and mass genocide that claimed the lives of an estimated 1,000,000 people. Prior to the conflict, Emmanuel was a businessman and a local Pastor of small church that fed the poor every week. Just like other Christians that move in the supernatural, Emmanuel practiced praying and fasting on a regular basis. When the civil war broke out, Emmanuel was caught in the crossfire of an attack. An RPG (rocket propelled grenade) hit the building he was standing next to. He survived the blast and was rushed to the hospital. The doctors were discussing protocol to amputate his arm due to the shrapnel ripping away some of the flesh . But when they saw his midsection they decided he may not be alive long enough. Part of Emmanuel's intestines were hanging out of his belly. Although Emmanuel bravely held them in with his own hand, doctors feared the worst. They transferred him to another hospital because the doctors decided they needed to focus their resources on patients that will live. (This is common practice amongst doctors in war zones.)*

Since the fighting intensified, Emmanuel ended up at a makeshift hospital inside a school. The hospital he was supposed to be transferred to was overcrowded with patients. The makeshift hospital at the school was eventually overrun by men with machine guns and machetes. The doctors and nurses ran for their lives. The men with guns left Emmanuel and the other mortally wounded people for dead. Emmanuel was rescued two weeks later. He had barely any water, no air conditioning, no medicine, but he had God. Members of the medical community around the world are baffled when they hear Emmanuel's story of survival. Doctors argue that Emmanuel should of died within three days because of the lack of water and infection. It was common knowledge that when the rebels raided a hospital it was stripped of all medical supplies and food. Emmanuel survived on prayer and fasting. It was his spiritual fitness that overtook his physical fitness. His survival is commonly called impossible but the bible says:

> But Jesus beheld them, and said unto them, With men this is impossible; but with God all things are possible. (Matthew 19:26)

The Common Thread

Perhaps you may have picked up on the common thread throughout these testimonies. If you missed it, then let me enlighten to you the power of fasting. Fasting is the practice of abstaining from food for certain periods of time. The practice of fasting is the thread that ties many of the stories in this book together. Fasting is a method used by many people in the bible to gain spiritual strength. If more preppers of the Christian faith practiced fasting they would understand that it is the ultimate prep. The practice of fasting literally can take you from being a victim to being a victor. Jesus Christ practiced fasting and expected his followers to do the same:

> 17But thou, when thou fastest, anoint thine head, and wash thy face;

18That thou appear not unto men to fast, but unto thy Father which is in secret: and thy Father, which seeth in secret, shall reward thee openly.
(Matthew 6:17-18)

An example of God rewarding you when you fast is supernatural events happening in your life. The apostle Paul was a man that fasted often. God used him to write a large portion of the New Testament scriptures. However, Paul was so spiritually strong that demon possessed people would get healed the moment he told the demon to leave. In the physical world, when he was bitten by a poisonous snake he simply ignored it like a common bug. The bible recorded the event in the book of Acts:

3And when Paul had gathered a bundle of sticks, and laid them on the fire, there came a viper out of the heat, and fastened on his hand.
4And when the barbarians saw the venomous beast hang on his hand, they said among themselves, No doubt this man is a murderer, whom, though he hath escaped the sea, yet vengeance suffereth not to live.
5And he shook off the beast into the fire, and felt no harm.
6Howbeit they looked when he should have swollen, or fallen down dead suddenly: but after they had looked a great while, and saw no harm come to him, they changed their minds, and said that he was a god.

Think about this for a second. The natives on the island should be well aware of the poisonous snakes because they lived there for generations. Venomous snakes tend to hang on to its prey because they are injecting their venom in a thorough manner. So even though Paul was as juiced as a bodybuilder from the snakes needles, he didn't show any swelling, feverish symptoms, or keel over and die like other people. Since fasting builds your trust in God, fear no longer overtakes you. Paul was fearless when the snake bit him. He through it in the fire like it was a harmless worm.

Most people I know would have been freaking out saying, "Help me, call 911, I have been bit by a snake!" But the apostle Paul was not like most people and the honest truth is that most people will not fast. The Apostle Paul's outer strength was fortified by his inner strength. That inner strength came from his relationship with Christ and his private practice of fasting.

Do you recognize the following names listed below:

Moses, Jesus Christ, Martin Luther, Mother Teresa, Mohandas Gandhi, King David, George Washington, John Wesley, Queen Ester, Dr. Martin Luther King Jr., and Cesar Chavez?

These were all people that changed the course of history during the course of their lives. The common thread that weaves them all together is that they all practiced fasting from food. In their lifetime, many of these people faced every fear the common prepper of today faced: War, plagues, starvation, famine, civil unrest, economic collapse, martial law, natural disasters, corruption and the fight for freedom.

The practice of fasting is the ultimate prep for the preparedness community because one day there will be no access to food on a regular basis. It will give you spiritual strength to stand on the Word of God during a time of famine. While other people will easily lose focus due to a lack of food, your mind will remain sharp and your resolve will stay strong. The miracles I mentioned in this chapter were from people that fasted and it appears that the historical figures knew the same secret. It was there spiritual strength that enabled them to leave a mark in history. So I finish this chapter with this conclusion: If every prepper reading this book begins to focus on their inner strength; perhaps, and I do mean just perhaps; we too can make history.

Sources
*Seven Days In Heaven by Emmanuel Twagirimana

(**Author's note**: Emmanuel claimed to have died and came back to life. Though his story is believed by many, the medical community remained doubtful. However, they agree that his ability to stay alive for 2 weeks with his intestines exposed and no medical treatment is nothing short of a miracle. Although I know him personally and believe his story, I will encourage you to read his book called **Seven Days In Heaven by Emmanuel Twagirimana** to come to your own conclusion. I can say this much, I personally have seen this man perform miracles!)

Chapter 8

Animal Authority OR Authority over Animals?

I remember watching the movie "I am Legend" starring Will Smith a few years ago. This movie showed the reality of a highly contagious man made virus getting out of control in a populated area such as New York City. As the city became deserted over time, the animals in the Bronx zoo eventually broke free. The film showed lions roaming the heavily wooded areas of Central Park as well as hunting in the city streets. Wild animals escaping captivity during a crisis is not reserved for Hollywood.

In 1992, Hurricane Andrew arrived in South Florida and caused 26 billion dollars worth of damage. In the process of destroying homes, the hurricane damaged many exotic pet facilities including the Metro Zoo. Numerous animals died during the storm but some managed to escape to freedom in the nearby everglades. Many of the animals were never captured.

When the grid goes down in the United States, people will have to contend with animals from every sector. Human beings will have to deal with the escaped pride of lions from the local zoo or the aggressive wild boars that roam throughout the southern United States. Perhaps you will have to deal with the grizzly bears in the Pacific Northwest or the mountain lions roaming the woods from California to Georgia. (Yes, they have been spotted in Georgia!)

Most preppers will tell you that if they come across a large animal in the wild they will simply shoot it. Sounds simple right? If you ask any skilled hunter, it does not always work that way. Yes, at times you may get the drop on an animal and be able to pick him off from 150 yards, but there is always a high level of skill involved. You must be extremely quiet, have great marksmanship, and manage to keep the animal from smelling your presence in the wind. This is another section of the book where I want to force the survivalist/prepper to be honest with himself. Chances are, if you are not a skilled hunter, the role may be reversed. In a grid down situation, a dangerous animal may stalk you. He may even invite a few friends to join him for prepper a la carte.

In a grid down situation, even a pack of wild dogs will become a serious threat. These animals will be abandoned and hungry. There will be no dog catchers or animal control to call. If they surround your child they will show no empathy. The dogs will rely on their instinct to feed their hungry bellies.

I can recall one such event in my youth. My older brother was about 14 years old and I was 5. We were living in upstate New York at the time and we enjoyed my mother's decision to move to the quiet neighborhood with abundant wildlife. That all changed one day as my brother and I walked home from the playground. A pack of dogs surrounded us and became very aggressive. My brother immediately found a big stick and began to beat them away. One of the dogs actually attacked me as my older brother was preoccupied with the other dogs. It seemed like the mutt was actually trying to drag me into the woods! My brother beat the devil's dog off of me but he sustained a few bite marks from the other mutts in the process. This experience as a child has always made me ponder this question: what if this happened when it becomes abandoned dogs that haven't eaten in a week? I think the situation would become a fight to the death.

Suppose you have to bug out to the woods in an emergency situation and you encounter a mountain lion while unarmed? It could be a situation as simple as you leaving camp to go use the bath room and you leave your pistol in camp. This 250 pound cat smelled the deer steaks you guys were cooking and decided to stalk the camp to get a free meal. The cat was just going to wait until you guys were sleeping to come out and steal food from your backpacks. While waiting in the bush, Patti the prepper goes to a nearby bush to relieve herself. The hungry cat goes to investigate and gets in a stare down with Patti. If Patti knows her true authority as a child of the living God, she should be able to command this cat to go back into the woods without breaking a sweat. I will give you few examples of this defiant act of faith.

From an excerpt of his book "Like a Mighty Wind", Christian author and missionary Mel Tari tells of miraculous encounters with animals in the jungles of Indonesia – a network of islands in the Pacific Ocean. In one account he wrote:

My sister and a brother in the Lord work for the Lord in the jungles of Sumatra. Many times they must cross rivers. One day this brother went to cross the river. He could not swim and the water came to his waist as it was flood time. The Moslems and pagans stood on the bank and laughed.

"Ha, ha", they said. "This is the day for him to die."

As he was struggling to get across the river, crocodiles came toward him to swallow him. When they were three or four feet away from him, they were ready to use their tails to crush him. When crocodiles hit with their tails they can knock canoes in half. So when they come at a man, he has absolutely no power to protect himself.

Suddenly this brother remembered Mark 16:18. As he stood there in the river, he said, "Crocodiles, in the name of Jesus I command you to leave."

The crocodiles came another foot closer, then, swish, they turned around and swam away. The Moslems and the pagans stood on the bank of the river and said, "We've never seen anything like this. The crocodiles obeyed that man."
(Like a Mighty Wind p.35)

Jesus said in Mark 16:18 "They shall take up serpents and if they drink any deadly thing it shall not hurt them;" I do not advocate picking up dangerous animals of any kind for show and tell because Jesus also clearly says, "Do not tempt the Lord thy God" in Luke 4:12. What He means is that believers in Him have an absolute authority over the animal kingdom. Jesus proved this when He rode an unbroken colt in Luke 19:30-35. Most ranchers around the world will tell you that riding an unbroken colt is extremely dangerous because the animal will sometimes buck and kick like a rodeo show. Yet Jesus made the animal become supernaturally docile with no formal training.

In the book of Genesis, God actually tells Adam that he is to have dominion over every animal. HE says in Genesis 1:28 "and have dominion over the fish of the sea, and over the fowl of the air, and over every living thing that moveth upon the earth." Well if Jesus is biblically recognized as the second Adam, and he also proved his mastery over the animals, shouldn't we be doing the same?

Jesus did say to his followers, "Verily, verily, I say unto you, He that believeth on me, the works that I do shall he do also; and greater works than these shall he do; because I go unto my Father." (John 14:12)

Keep this promise in mind because Jesus showed us He can make fishermen pull in the biggest load of fish during a fishing expedition, force a herd of swine into the sea, ride an unbroken colt, and multiply fish to feed thousands of people. (Matt. 8:30-32, Luke 5:5-7, Matt. 14:13-21)

As a pastor I naturally believe these things are possible, yet as a prepper I have to put my beliefs into practice. One day I was painting an outside porch and deck at the home of a Christian lady named Gloria. We had a conversation about snakes and she said, "Brother Keith, I can't stand snakes. Do you think we can pray them off my property?" I agreed to do so with her and we walked her entire property boundary line praying for God to remove the snakes from her property. As we were finishing our prayers over the property, the Holy Spirit led me to say "Furthermore to any serpent that refuses to listen to the word of the LORD, that refuses to leave this property, I curse you to the birds of the air to be eaten for your disobedience!"

The very next day I was standing on a ladder painting part of the outer deck when something flew quickly in my peripheral vision. I figured it was just a bird so I paid it no mind. I then noticed a second bird fly quickly past my view so I took notice of the bird's flight plan. He landed in Gloria's yard next to a 3 foot long shiny object. To my amazement, three birds were plucking at a snake in the lawn! The snake was crawling at top speed to escape the pecking on his slithery body. The bird's were treating this serpent like a common worm and I nearly fell off the ladder in laughter yelling "Hallelujah!".

A local handyman named Bart experienced dominion over the animals. One day he was working outdoors in a customer's yard. A large black bear came in the yard to feast on the customer's garden. Bart looked at the approaching bear and said, "In the name of Jesus Christ, I command you to go back into the forest!" The bear simply turned around and walked back into the dense foliage.

God can use animals to punish you

Karma. I have heard it said by people all over the world. In many of the Eastern religions of the world it defines one's actions, deeds or intentions. According to the online dictionary Wikipedia, good intent and good deed contribute to good karma and future happiness, while bad intent and bad deed contribute to bad karma and future suffering. Perhaps karma is a universal law instilled by the Creator because many other religions seem to recognize this particular belief system.

Written in 1500 BC, the oldest book of the Bible says "Even as I have seen, they that plow iniquity, and sow wickedness, reap the same." (Job 4:8)

Interestingly enough, through the same Holy inspiration, the Apostle Paul writes in the book of Galatians Chapter 6 Verse 7: "Be not deceived; God is not mocked: for whatsoever a man soweth, that shall he also reap ". Many people in the English speaking secular world have used this scripture to coin the term "what goes around comes around".

Do you remember the terrorist group Boko Haram kidnapping 276 school girls in Northern Nigeria with plans to sell them into slavery? This terrorist act was reported worldwide and to this date some of the girls still remain missing. I recall Christians worldwide began praying for the return of the little girls and for God to bring the men responsible to justice. A few weeks later in the June 26, 2014 issue of Nigeria's Vanguard Newspaper it was reported that many of the men from Boko Haram were being attacked by poisonous snakes and killer bees. The terrorist group began to suffer mass casualties due to the eerie attacks at an alarming rate. As a result, many of the perpetrators began to flee to the neighboring country Cameroon hoping to escape the onslaught of snakes and bees. One captured member of the terror organization has said, "most of us are fleeing because there are too many snakes and bees now in the forest. Once they bite, they disappear and the victims do not last for 24 hours".

And the LORD sent fiery serpents among the people, and they bit the people; and much people of Israel died. (Numbers 21:6)

Here is my point for my friends in the prepper community: Do not think your preps will stop karma from biting you in the asymmetric lower back side of your body. God will even use a wild animal to punish someone. There are some preppers that have routinely stolen things from people in business deals as well as preppers that are eager to conduct themselves with the most vile behavior in the event of a societal collapse. If you have someone like this within your preparedness community may I suggest you cut ties with them now. Having a clean conscious and a good moral character will be a key ingredient for surviving the days ahead.

Now I beseech you, brethren, mark them which cause divisions and offences contrary to the doctrine which ye have learned; and avoid them.
(Romans 16:17)

God can use an animal to protect you

We all know that a trained animal can protect a human. Special dogs are used by law enforcement and people with special handicaps all the time. I believe that God uses untrained animals to protect people too. This is something that folks of a preparedness mindset should embrace. There are countless stories of people drowning in the ocean and a dolphin saves them.

There is evidence that God used untrained wild animals to help protect the first prepper in history. In one of the books that did not make it into the final compilation of the Bible, there are some verses that actually record this event. The book of Jasher is mentioned in the King James Bible on two different occasions:

Also he bade them teach the children of Judah the use of the bow: behold, it is written in the book of Jasher. (2 Samuel 2:18)

And the sun stood still, and the moon stayed, until the people had avenged themselves upon their enemies. Is not this written in the

book of Jasher? So the sun stood still in the midst of heaven, and hasted not to go down about a whole day.
(Joshua 10:13)

For those of you that don't remember me mentioning the law of Moses that states "out of the mouth of two or three witnesses a matter is established", I suggest you refer to my chapter titled "Multiple Confirmations".

Using this law, I had a Hebrew Scholar loan me his copy of the book of Jasher. Although he felt his copy is legitimate, I will advise that there is a huge debate among scholars worldwide about the authenticity of this lost book. The following passage answered my question regarding the security of Noah's family when their neighbors began to panic. The book of Jasher chapter 6 verses 16 thru 25 gives the following portrayal of animals protecting Noah:

16 And all the sons of men that were left upon the earth, became exhausted through evil on account of the rain, for the waters were coming more violently upon the earth, and the animals and beasts were still surrounding the ark.
17 And the sons of men assembled together, about seven hundred thousand men and women, and they came unto Noah to the ark.
18 And they called to Noah, saying, Open for us that we may come to thee in the ark--and wherefore shall we die?
19 And Noah, with a loud voice, answered them from the ark, saying, Have you not all rebelled against the Lord, and said that he does not exist? and therefore the Lord brought upon you this evil, to destroy and cut you off from the face of the earth.
20 Is not this the thing that I spoke to you of one hundred and twenty years back, and you would not hearken to the voice of the Lord, and now do you desire to live upon earth?
21 And they said to Noah, We are ready to return to the Lord; only open for us that we may live and not die.
22 And Noah answered them, saying, Behold now that you see the trouble of your souls, you wish to return to the Lord; why did you not

return during these hundred and twenty years, which the Lord granted you as the determined period?
23 But now you come and tell me this on account of the troubles of your souls, now also the Lord will not listen to you, neither will he give ear to you on this day, so that you will not now succeed in your wishes.
24 And the sons of men approached in order to break into the ark, to come in on account of the rain, for they could not bear the rain upon them.
25 And the Lord sent all the beasts and animals that stood round the ark. And the beasts overpowered them and drove them from that place, and every man went his way and they again scattered themselves upon the face of the earth.

Since my detractors will like to argue that this book holds no biblical value, I would like to point out the other hero in the book of Numbers from the Bible. Obviously, God almighty and Moses are the principle characters for the book of Numbers, but a lesser known hero remains: The donkey.

The disobedient Prophet Balaam was riding his donkey to go do some mischief. God sent an Angel with a sword to kill Balaam as he was going down a narrow alley. Since the Angel was invisible to the human eye, Balaam was walking to his death without knowing it. His donkey had the ability to see into the other light spectrum and took evasive action to save Balaam's life:

22 And God's anger was kindled because he went: and the angel of the Lord stood in the way for an adversary against him. Now he was riding upon his ass, and his two servants were with him.

23 And the ass saw the angel of the Lord standing in the way, and his sword drawn in his hand: and the ass turned aside out of the way,

and went into the field: and Balaam smote the ass, to turn her into the way.

²⁴ But the angel of the Lord stood in a path of the vineyards, a wall being on this side, and a wall on that side.

²⁵ And when the ass saw the angel of the Lord, she thrust herself unto the wall, and crushed Balaam's foot against the wall: and he smote her again.

²⁶ And the angel of the Lord went further, and stood in a narrow place, where was no way to turn either to the right hand or to the left.

²⁷ And when the ass saw the angel of the Lord, she fell down under Balaam: and Balaam's anger was kindled, and he smote the ass with a staff.

²⁸ And the Lord opened the mouth of the ass, and she said unto Balaam, What have I done unto thee, that thou hast smitten me these three times?

²⁹ And Balaam said unto the ass, Because thou hast mocked me: I would there were a sword in mine hand, for now would I kill thee.

³⁰ And the ass said unto Balaam, Am not I thine ass, upon which thou hast ridden ever since I was thine unto this day? was I ever wont to do so unto thee? and he said, Nay.

³¹ Then the LORD opened the eyes of Balaam, and he saw the angel of the LORD standing in the way, and his sword drawn in his hand: and he bowed down his head, and fell flat on his face.

³² And the angel of the LORD said unto him, Wherefore hast thou smitten thine ass these three times? behold, I went out to withstand thee, because thy way is perverse before me:

³³ And the ass saw me, and turned from me these three times: unless she had turned from me, surely now also I had slain thee, and saved her alive.

Did I make my point yet? An animal can protect a human being in the most diverse situation and at times in a God ordained manner. Other times the animal can protect someone out of the interest of self preservation. I believe the preppers need to start building a relationship with God first and then the animals He has provided for us.

God can send animals to deliver a warning

Many people will agree with me that guard dogs give warnings when an intruder is on their property. People will say it's because the dog is simply protecting his master or the dog has been trained well. But what about the cases when it is a wild animal providing the warning? Take for instance the 2004 Asian Tsunami that devastated the coastlines of many countries. There are countless stories of wild animals as well as house trained creatures running to the high grounds an hour before the tsunami made landfall. The people that understood this to be a warning sign of danger to come, immediately followed the animals to the higher grounds inland.

Speaking of waves and tsunamis; do you remember the original prepper Noah? In the book of Genesis Chapter 8 we must take notice of Noah's flood warning system. Since the world was covered with water, Noah had to use birds to check for safety. The Bible records him using a raven and a dove since he didn't have the weather channel on his plasma television. He sent them out a few different times to warn him of flash floods. The last thing Noah needed was to leave his cruise ship too early with random tsunami's still flooding the area. Eventually the birds stopped returning to the ark, thus letting Noah know that the floods had receded.

Still not convinced? Let me help you remember the showdown between Moses and the King of Egypt aka Pharaoh. In the biblical story of Exodus, Moses on the behalf of God, goes before the King of Egypt to demand the release of the Hebrew people. Pharaoh refuses to let his entire slave work force go free so Moses begins a series of warnings and plagues. Moses first used a snake in Pharaoh's courtyard to deliver the warning, but that first attempt proved unfruitful because Pharaoh did not heed the warning. Moses then sends swarms of frogs into the homes and condominiums throughout Egypt. Pharaoh takes heed to the warning and then asks Moses to get rid of the frogs. Moses asks God to help with the cleanup service and the frogs leave the people's nice homes. Pharaoh then decides to play hardball and refuses to let the slaves go despite being warned of the consequences. Moses then sends in a swarm of lice to make the citizens of Egypt miserable. Pharaoh notices that he is losing political popularity then decides to heed Moses warning and agrees to let the slaves go. Moses asks God to remove the lice and life goes back to normal until Pharaoh decides to ignore the last warning and backs out of the deal. So Moses then sends flies and the entire process repeats. Moses then has to resort to sending locusts to destroy the country's agriculture and the entire process repeats. God used snakes, frogs, lice, and locusts to deliver warnings to the King of Egypt before resorting to heavy handed tactics like hail storms and the Angel of Death. (Exodus Chapters 8-12)

God using an animal as a warning indicator could be very subtle, like the time I saw a massive 400 pound wild boar on the side of the road in North Georgia on the way to my job in Atlanta. Wild boar of this size generally tend to stay deep in the forest where they cannot be detected by humans. However, this one stood at the side of the highway for me to look at him. As I slowed the car down to look at the massive beast in his dark red eyes, he glared back at me as if taunting me, and then disappeared into the bushes. I knew in my spirit that something was afoot. Sure enough, there was a false allegation stirred up about me at my job and I was fired the very next day.

Sometimes the warning signs are not so subtle. A good friend of mine and fellow prepper named Bryce encountered this in college. During his tenure at Western Carolina University, Bryce was leaving the dorm rooms and moving off campus for his senior year. He found two different guys, both with a house off campus desiring a responsible roommate. Although he was a Christian, Bryce was leaning towards moving in with the guy that was the party animal. Bryce's dad told him to move in with the other guy in order to get more work done. Bryce knew his dad was right, but wanted to have a better social life for his senior year. Against his better judgment, Bryce decided to drive to the party animal's house to tell him personally that he would accept his offer to move in. On his way to the guy's house, a bat measuring 2 feet in length planted itself on the windshield while Bryce was driving. Bryce screamed in terror as the animal finally freed itself from the pressure of the wind. Taking this is a warning sign, Bryce immediately turned the vehicle around and decided to move in with the more reserved student. Bryce enjoyed his final year of college with no more incidents. Unfortunately, the young man that took Bryce's place as the roommate with the party animal didn't share the same sentiment or outcome. Bryce's replacement went with the party animal to go boozing on liquor while white water rafting one weather friendly weekend. The party animal was supposed to watch over his drunk roommate but failed miserably since he was drunk as well. The young man that replaced Bryce drowned to death during the outing. His body was finally found a week later.

If any of you lack wisdom, let him ask of God, that giveth to all men liberally, and upbraideth not; and it shall be given him.
(James 1:5)

God can use animals in a dream to deliver a warning

If you're prepping, but your spiritual senses are dull, I think you are at a big disadvantage. The Bible says "if any man lacks wisdom, let him ask of God…" I take careful notice of everything around me including animals in my dreams. Why not? In the Bible, Joseph did the same thing when he interpreted the King of Egypt's dream. For those of you not familiar with this story, the King of Egypt had a dream of seven well fed cows. Then he saw seven malnourished cows sitting on the side of the river. To the King's horror, the seven malnourished cows came and ate the seven well fed cows. Joseph was summoned before the King to tell him the meaning of the dream and Joseph told him that Egypt would have seven great years of agriculture and wealth, but after that, they would have seven years of famine and depression. (Genesis 41)

Recently, I had a dream that made me wonder why God give it to me. It wasn't until writing this book that it made sense. I've come across some preppers that feel there is a religious persecution coming rivaling the atrocities committed by the Nazi's during World War II. They say that history repeats itself, so you be the judge. In this dream, I was in a high speed chase with some goons that wanted to kill me for being a pastor that preaches about

Jesus. The chase was pretty intense and I somehow managed to evade them and get them off my tail. I ended up driving for hours through large mountains and jungle terrain. Eventually, I found a house with a big driveway somewhere in the middle of nowhere. As I parked the car, I couldn't help the feeling of being watched. The house was surrounded by forest so I couldn't see through the thick brush. As I walked to the porch, full grown African lions began to surround me and the vehicle. They blocked me from running onto the porch and from running down the driveway. I quickly ran back to my car, closed the doors and began winding the windows up. One of the lions quickly stuck his paw in the back window to keep me from winding it up. Terrified I began fumbling with my keys to start the car. While I was fumbling, one of the lions cleverly used his teeth to lift the door handle on the back door, meanwhile another lion intelligently used his paw to open the passenger door handle. Fearing the worst, I closed my eyes and prayed fervently. One of the lions took the keys to the car in his mouth and walked away. The other lion grabbed me by my shirt and dragged me out of the car. Still praying aloud, I opened my eyes and noticed a pastor on the porch. He signaled for me to walk to the porch. I stood to my feet and the lions made a ceremonial aisle with their bodies for me to walk past. I kept praying as I walked by them, eventually making it to the porch. The pastor on the porch told the lions, "Its okay boys, he is one of us!" The lions broke rank and began to walk back into the dense forest surrounding the house. The pastor opened the front door and I saw Christians cowering in fear. The pastor told everyone, "It's okay, he's one of us." Everyone breathed a sigh of relief.

And it shall come to pass in the last days, saith God, I will pour out of my Spirit upon all flesh: and your sons and your daughters shall prophesy, and your young men shall see visions, and your old men shall dream dreams:
(Acts 2:17)

Chapter 9

The Ultimate Bug Out Vehicle

(Author's Note: The following words you are about to read may be absolutely unbelievable to some or an experienced truth for others. If you have a lack of faith or a spirit of unbelief, I highly suggest you skip this chapter. However, if you are one of those people that believe that anything is possible with God, then this chapter is for you. I also pray that God almighty will bless you with the faith to pray for these experiences when tough times come.)

Before we dig into this chapter, it is important that you familiarize yourself with some popular words in the emergency preparedness world. They may be considered slang words to some of you readers, but these are commonly used words among preppers:

Bug Out- According to the online website urbandictionary.com the term "bug out" means to retreat or flee especially in a panic during a battle. In a non-military use, it means to depart quickly. The term originated among United States servicemen during the Korean War (1950-1953) and then leaked into civilian culture. Now in 2015 the term is commonly used among preppers throughout the world. Preppers in Europe as well as the United States use the term when describing their plan of escape when calamity hits.

Bug Out Vehicle- This term usually refers to the mode of transportation you will use during your great escape from a disaster or crisis. For example: When Hurricane Katrina approached New Orleans, many people drove their cars hundreds of miles inland. The vehicles each individual drove would be considered a bug out vehicle.

A friend of mine had recently emailed me a link to watch of an expensive bug out vehicle. This specialized truck had the appearance of an SUV, but it came with all the fixings. It had the ability to use unleaded gasoline or diesel fuel. Solar panels were attached to the top to power your electronics. Even though the vehicle had 4 wheel drive, it also had the ability to drive in 4 feet of water without stalling. There was also a makeshift kitchen, fold out sleeping area, and fishing equipment attached to the exterior.

As much as I liked the vehicle, I have seen enough videos of mobs of angry people overpowering a vehicle; especially when people are desperate. Now don't get me wrong, the vehicle I described above would be great for a camping trip, but some of these souped up bug out vehicles can also be a deathtrap. Many preppers are now investing in smaller modes of transportation for this reason. Motorcycles, bicycles, and helicopters are becoming attractive to people looking to get out of Dodge. No matter which option you prefer, there will be positive and negative outcomes.

By observing the different modes of transportation and realizing that the scenarios could be different for everyone, I always knew in my spirit that there must be another mode of travel. The Bible says that "God is no respecter of persons", therefore I knew it wouldn't be like God to bless the rich guy with the helicopter to bring his family to safety, meanwhile a righteous yet poor family just has to stay put and endure the storm of events. By careful study of the Bible, testimonials from numerous people and a personal experience of my own, I realized that God has the ability to provide a supernatural mode of transportation. An example of this is found in the book of Acts:

38And he commanded the chariot to stand still: and they went down both into the water, both Philip and the eunuch; and he baptized him.

39And when they were come up out of the water, the Spirit of the Lord caught away Philip, that the eunuch saw him no more: and he went on his way rejoicing.
40But Philip was found at Azotus: and passing through he preached in all the cities, till he came to Caesarea.
(Acts 8:38-40)

There is a way of travel that requires some serious faith, but the speed by which you travel can be mind blowing. The biblical term for it is called Translation or to be Translated. It occurs when God supernaturally moves your physical or spiritual body to another place. This supernatural means of travel only happens when God sees fit for it to occur. In the passage mentioned above, Phillip the evangelist was teaching the Ethiopian Eunuch revelations of Jesus Christ. After the Bible study, Phillip decides to baptize the eunuch in some nearby water. Immediately after the baptism, Phillip disappears from the eunuch's presence and re-appears nearly 40 miles away in a place called Azotus without the use of a chariot or donkey.

If you can be faithful to God, these type of miracles may happen in your life, especially in an emergency situation. I am absolutely convinced that God is going to move people to different geographic locations on the earth to protect them during the biblical "last days". However, I know God is using this method now in the every day lives of his children.

God's Passing Lane

My friends David and Bonnie Hina were driving from North Carolina to Georgia one rainy day in spring. As they were driving down Highway I-985 by Gainesville, Georgia, the light rain became a monsoon. Cars were pulling over to the side of the highway due to the lack of visibility. Bonnie and David became nervous of the possibility of the big eighteen wheeler trucks losing control in the bizarre weather because it was common for eighteen wheelers to hit small cars in bad weather due to low visibility. The rain came down with more intensity and the couple began praying fervently for God to deliver them to safety. All of sudden, the vehicle felt like they were flying. The thick highway fog that remained around the vehicle suddenly gave way to sunlight. The heavy rain stopped and they realized they were driving on a dry highway south of Atlanta. David looked at his mileage counter in disbelief because they traveled a distance of 40 miles in less than 2 minutes. The couple began praising God and singing gospel songs to each other for the rest of their journey.

If an emergency happens in the future and your family has to drive through hellish conditions for safety, the knowledge of God providing supernatural travel can be a lifesaver. Even if you have been taken captive by some unsavory characters, God can supernaturally move you into another location like he did Phillip the evangelist.

One evening I was watching the Christian Broadcast Network and the story of a Pastor in Central America nearly made me fall out of my chair. The Pastor was preaching against the drug dealers ruining his local community. The local drug dealers decided that this Pastor must be killed for speaking against their business. One day they kidnapped him and locked him into the windowless bathroom of one of their local bars. While they were trying to decide a place to leave his body after killing him, the pastor closed his eyes and began to pray fervently for God to save him. When he opened his eyes he was standing in the middle of the street two blocks away! Obviously he lived to tell his story on Christian television, but I think God wanted the millions of people watching the television program to know that God can literally snatch you out of the jaws of death.

Can God use this method to warn me of danger?

He absolutely can! God supernaturally took a prophet named Ezekiel out of his physical body to show him the dangerous spiritual condition of Israel as well as some of the men perpetrating the illegal Satanic rituals:

³ And he put forth the form of an hand, and took me by a lock of mine head; and the spirit lifted me up between the earth and the heaven, and brought me in the visions of God to Jerusalem, to the door of the inner gate that looketh toward the north; where was the seat of the image of jealousy, which provoketh to jealousy.

⁴ And, behold, the glory of the God of Israel was there, according to the vision that I saw in the plain.

⁵ Then said he unto me, Son of man, lift up thine eyes now the way toward the north. So I lifted up mine eyes the way toward the north, and behold northward at the gate of the altar this image of jealousy in the entry.

⁶ He said furthermore unto me, Son of man, seest thou what they do? even the great abominations that the house of Israel committeth here, that I should go far off from my sanctuary? but turn thee yet again, and thou shalt see greater abominations.

⁷ And he brought me to the door of the court; and when I looked, behold a hole in the wall.

⁸ Then said he unto me, Son of man, dig now in the wall: and when I had digged in the wall, behold a door.

⁹ And he said unto me, Go in, and behold the wicked abominations that they do here.

¹⁰ So I went in and saw; and behold every form of creeping things, and abominable beasts, and all the idols of the house of Israel, portrayed upon the wall round about.

¹¹ And there stood before them seventy men of the ancients of the house of Israel, and in the midst of them stood Jaazaniah the son of Shaphan, with every man his censer in his hand; and a thick cloud of incense went up.

(Ezekiel 8:3-11)

As preppers, we think about situations such as a foreign terrorist group plotting to raid your neighborhood or maybe a gang of marauders planning to ransack your home. Wouldn't it be cool if there was a way to get advanced notice without the use of technology in a grid down situation? There is a way to do it but it will require discipline.

My friend Earl of Elberton, Georgia is one such man. A former professional boxer, Earl knew a thing or two about discipline. For years he followed a strict 5 am workout regimen to have the ability to fight opponents with lightning quick speed. So years later when he became a pastor, he was well seasoned with fighting crafty opponents. The next opponent he faced had the money and the resources to defeat him because it was prominent members of his community during the time of desegregation. Earl was being targeted for an ugly smear campaign by community leaders and church elders because of his willingness to integrate the churches with people of color. The members of his fellow Caucasian community decided to resort to violence to rid themselves of the righteous Pastor Earl. One evening as Earl was in prayer in his bedroom, he found himself floating in the air within the confines of a community leader's living room. Earl had somehow left his physical body but his spirit was observing a meeting concerning him. Earl witnessed the exact detail of the plan to frame him for crimes and possibly kill him. The conspirators mentioned the dates and times of their planned events enabling Earl to out maneuver their actions.

When the men realized their plans were not working, they became suspicious of each other and began to fight amongst themselves. They eventually broke their partnership apart and became bitter enemies. Earl realized that his disciplined prayer life helped him avoid the trap set for him. Through constant prayer, Earl had direct contact with his Creator. Just like the biblical prophet Ezekiel, God gave Earl supernatural foresight to evade his enemies on both the political and religious landscape.

Isolated Incident?

These are not isolated incidents. Numerous believers around the world have had similar God ordained experiences. Let me tell you what happened to me:

During the year 2012, I began to fervently pray for politicians in the United States as well as other world leaders. I questioned God on the true intentions of some of these men and women. Many of these world leaders seemed like well intentioned people, however when they took office, they all of a sudden seemed have a bad case of amnesia. It had gotten so bad that lower members of their political party questioned the irrational decision making that began to follow that leader. Now let me point out that I am not naive to all the conspiracy theories regarding some of the world leaders, trust me, some of these theories will be proven true on judgment day. But do people actually realize the demonic forces controlling some of these world leaders? I really don't think so.

One night, I went to sleep, only to find myself being taken to a deep underground base by an Angel. This place had massive caverns and tunnels that went to other places through the earth. There were massive giants walking around down there as well as a few humans. Since I was with the Angel, he seemed to keep some type of shield on me that made me invisible. I saw an ancient powerful witch in one of the caverns holding a board meeting with a few politicians from around the world. She was teaching the politicians some very powerful spells and enchantments to gain more political power in their respective governments by way of mass hypnosis and trickery. For some reason, I was not permitted to identify the world leaders in this wicked place. I suppose that was to protect me from blabbing their personal names to the world, but it was one of my personal experiences that bear witness to the biblical record of Ezekiel Chapter 8.

This experience of getting supernaturally translated taught me the most important thing about prepping for the future. There will be no political answer to solve the moral problems within the United States. The governmental problems we see in the natural world are a direct result of the spiritual battles. The Apostle Paul said in the book of Ephesians, "For we wrestle not against flesh and blood, but against principalities, against powers, against the rulers of the darkness of this world, against spiritual wickedness in high *places*." (Ephesians 6:12)

God will do it when He wants to!

In February 2015, I learned that a dear friend of my family had passed away in Jamaica. I felt in my spirit that I needed to be at that funeral to minister to some of the family members of the deceased.

I knew to leave to Jamaica on such notice would be problematic. There were multiple hurdles to be solved that seemed impossible to overcome.

1) I was scheduled the same weekend to assist with a healing meeting at my home church in North Carolina.
2) A last minute flight to Jamaica was going to cost $800. I did not want to borrow the money from anyone to go, including credit card companies.
3) My wife had to work on Thursday, so I had to babysit our children on the same Thursday, thus forcing me to take a flight on Friday.
4) The first problem with me flying to Jamaica on Friday was that I would need someone to drive me from my off the grid house to Atlanta airport which was a 2 and half hour ride. The second problem with me arriving to Jamaica on Friday is that I would need transportation to the wake/funeral services in a remote part of Jamaica. It was 2 hours by car from the Montego Bay, Jamaica airport to the funeral home, in addition to the 2 hour flight to Jamaica. These cab rides between the airports can be costly and time consuming.

Since I already experienced being supernaturally translated in the past I expected God to do the same for me. The Bible says that "faith without works is dead", so I decided to have my passport, my debit card, and some extra petty cash in my pocket for my supernatural trip. I even wore a summer shirt under my winter sweater just in case I would get too hot in the Jamaican sunshine. Are you ready to hear what happened next? Drum roll please…. Absolutely nothing. Nada. Zilch. No tropical mini-vacation during the cold winter. I thought God would whisk me away briefly to attend the funeral in Jamaica to console my loved ones and then zip me back to North Carolina. He didn't do it. Instead, he kept me in North Carolina to attend the healing meeting. At the healing meeting he used me to deliver a few people from some tormenting spirits as well as heal a young man from autism. The next day an ice storm came and knocked out electricity to my home. My wife and children needed me at the house during that deadly storm. If God had supernaturally taken me to Jamaica, the people that came to my church's healing meeting may not have been healed from depression, alcohol abuse, and autism. My family would have been left all alone in a power outage in freezing temperatures while I am sitting in sunny Jamaica. (And I would have felt responsible if anything happened to them in my absence.)

Even as a man of faith, I still go through lessons of trusting God with the steering wheel of my life. As much as I wanted to be in Jamaica with my close friends, the Lord knew that I did not need to be in Jamaica. His desire was for me to be in North Carolina to help set the captives free, not for me sipping a passion fruit punch on the beach. As believers in God, we have to learn to be obedient. As a prepper, we have to learn to trust. The preparedness community must learn to trust God in all aspects of their life, especially with supernatural provisions. There will be times where you will not have the means of transportation available to go where you want to be. However, if you ask God to "let His will be done", you will always be pleased at the outcome.

The topic of translation is a touchy subject. Some believe it, meanwhile others don't. I advise you to search the Bible thoroughly to see if I am telling you the truth or if I am a heretic from the hood (Hood is a slang term for inner city, black neighborhood, etc.). Satan worshippers and certain New Age groups are well aware of this method of transportation. They dub the term astral projection. I do not advise any reader of this book or any follower of Jesus Christ to study any New Age practice of astral projection. If you do, you will be subject to the demons you may encounter because you are not doing it with the approval of God almighty. Supernatural travel for Christians requires obedience to God and letting HIM decide when it is best for you.

Chapter 10

AR-15 or an Angel?

For those of that do not know, an AR-15 is a rifle. This weapon is the civilian version of the M-16 or M4 rifles used by military forces around the world. Here in the United States you can find them on sale at your local Walmart or sporting goods store. Due to their superb accuracy and light weight, they are used for target sports, hunting, and home defense.

This rifle is a preferred defensive weapon amongst law enforcement agencies across the United States as well as people in the preparedness community. Many in the preparedness community like the fact that the ammunition is plentiful and repairs for these rifles can be done rather quickly. Most preppers agree that if World War III were to begin between the United States and foreign powers, American citizens will be able to find parts for these guns very easily in order to defend themselves.

As a pastor, let me point out the fact that the AR-15 is nothing more than the sword of the day. Centuries ago, a sword was used to bring peace or conduct war. It was used to kill the lion coming to steal the farmer's sheep or it was used by the robber to kill the farmer before stealing his sheep.

My concern for people both today and in the coming years is that the robber coming to steal their souls. As preppers, we tend to focus on owning guns rather than on the consequences that will happen if we use it incorrectly. Another point of concern I have is for the preppers of the Christian persuasion who display a dependency on guns rather than a dependency on God's army with guns. I am speaking of Angels and not the fat little babies with wings in classical Italian paintings. (Which, by the way are not even biblical!)

During a period of fasting I encountered an Angel that was as tall as a professional basketball player yet he was built like a professional body builder. The serious tone on his face was enough to get a serial killer to confess the locations of his victims. I mean this dude was intimidating! Through my years living in Miami and New York, I have met gangsters and drug dealers alike. They could put fear in you to a certain degree but there was always the chance of knowing you could beat him to the punch or to the trigger (if needed). I felt the same way when I encountered Post Traumatic Stress Disorder in military men including a former Green Beret, and a former British SAS. There was always the belief in me that if this confrontation gets physical, I may leave with my life. However, when in the presence of a real life warrior Angel sent from the throne of God, your understanding of physical warfare becomes obsolete. I knew that if I gave that Angel any lip service, it could be curtains on the show called my life.

During my research for this book I stumbled across a testimony from a Satan worshipper that encountered an Angel. An ex-high priestess wrote named Elaine wrote:

"It was during that last visit to California that one of the incidents happened that started me on the road to accepting Christ, started me questioning Satan's claim to being more powerful than God. The high priest gathered a number of us together and told us that there was a family nearby who had been interfering with Satan. They had been converting a number of the cult members to the enemy, Jesus Christ, and were making a nuisance of themselves. Satan had given the order for them all to be killed. The high priest told us that we were all to go together in our spirit bodies (astral project), and kill them. So, we sat down in a circle with our candles in front of us and consciously left our bodies going in our spirits to the house to destroy these people. I was not at all enthusiastic about the project,

but had no choice. If I had disobeyed I would have been killed. Much to our surprise, as we arrived at the edge of this family's property, we could go no further. The whole area was surrounded by huge angels. The angels stood side by side holding hands. They were dressed in long white robes and stood so close together that their shoulders touched. They had no armor or weapons. Nobody could get through them, no matter how we tried. Any kind of weapon used merely bounced off of them doing them no harm. They laughed at us at first, daring us to come ahead and try to get through them. The other cult members got more furious with each passing moment. Suddenly their countenance changed and the fierce look from their eyes made all of us fall backwards onto the ground. A very humbling experience, I might add! I will never forget--as I sat on the ground looking up at them, one of the angels looked directly into my eyes and said to me in the most loving voice I had ever heard, "Won't you please accept Jesus as your Lord? If you pursue the course you are taking you will be destroyed. Satan really hates you, but Jesus loves you so much that He died for you. Please consider turning your life over to Jesus." That was the end of the battle for me. I refused to try any longer to get through. I was very shaken. The others tried for a while longer, but none succeeded. I doubt the family ever knew of the battle going on outside their house. They were completely protected! We called this particular type of special angels "link angels." Absolutely nothing can get through them. I was secretly thankful that we did not get through and the link angels had given me much to think about."

(**He Came to Set the Captives Free**, *by Rebecca Brown, MD p. 56-57)**

Angels on guard duty

Most preppers I know have began the process of securing their homes and properties for perilous times. Many have purchased state of the art alarm systems to protect their homes and cars. I urge them not to depend on these fancy alarm systems because they may not always be there. However, if your heart is right with God, He will most certainly be there. Jesus tells His believers in the gospels, "I will never leave you nor forsake you". I figure if Jesus doesn't leave, neither will His angels. In Billy Graham's 1975 book **Angels: God's Secret Agents**, there was a story of Angel's on guard duty:

The Reverend John G. Paton, pioneer missionary in the New Hebrides Islands, told a thrilling story involving the protective care of angels. Hostile natives surrounded his mission headquarters one night, intent on burning the Patons out and killing them. John Paton and his wife prayed all during that terror-filled night that God would deliver them. When daylight came they were amazed to see that, unaccountably, the attackers had left. They thanked God for delivering them. A year later, the chief of the tribe was converted to Jesus Christ, and Mr. Paton, remembering what had happened, asked the chief what had kept him and his men from burning down the house and killing them. The chief replied in surprise, "Who were all those men you had with you there?" The missionary answered, "There were no men there; just my wife and I." The chief argued that they had seen many men standing guard - hundreds of big men in shining garments with drawn swords in their hands. They seemed to circle the mission station so that the natives were afraid to attack. Only then did Mr. Paton realize that God had sent His angels to protect them. The chief agreed that there was no other explanation. Could it be that God had sent a legion of angels to protect His servants, whose lives were being endangered?
(Angels: God's Secret Agents *p. 5).***

With that experience, along with the experiences of other people, I have decided to enlist the use of Angels as my ultimate prepping weapon. Why not? In the book of Isaiah, God sent one lone Angel to defeat an army of 185,000 men:

Then the angel of the LORD went forth, and smote in the camp of the Assyrians a hundred and fourscore and five thousand: and when they arose early in the morning, behold, they were all dead corpses.

(Isaiah 37:36)

Okay, I know some of you are saying, "Come on Pastor, do you really expect me to believe that?" It's not my job to make you believe the events recorded in the Bible, because not everyone does. My job is to increase the faith of the people that do believe and to enlighten them on additional options for their prepping endeavors. There are people reading this book living on a fixed income with no financial means of hiring a security team for their apartment or house. However, if the faith of this person is strong enough to trust God in the bad times, then HE can send Angels to enable them to see brighter days. Preppers need to know that they can ask God to send some Angels to help them out.

Row, row, row your boat...

I know a hunter named Jim in North Carolina. (Name changed for security purposes.) One night he decided to get the jump on the other hunters before hunting season officially began. Jim set out by himself to hunt a prized animal. Since he was a few days early of the hunting season ordinance, he decided to row his boat upstream to his favorite hunting spot deep in the forest to avoid the pesky forest rangers. Once he was on foot, the plan was to wait under the full moon with the infra red scope for the target. Unfortunately, the forest rangers built the nerve to venture deep in the forest that night. They immediately ran after him, but they were slowed down because of the forest landscape. Jim began to run through the forest with his flashlight, hoping to get to his boat. Jim felt a sharp pain in his leg and assumed he hit a huge thorn bush. He ran faster to ditch the forest rangers. When he knew he lost them, he decided to examine his leg. To his shock, a rattlesnake was hanging off his lower leg! He unhinged the creature from his leg and crushed its head on some rocks. Then Jim began to feel really sick and dizzy. As any experienced hunter knows, snake bites require immediate attention and victims are to remain still to keep the venom from traveling. Jim knew he was in a life threatening situation because he just run half a mile at full speed through the forest and hastily got into his rowboat. The snake had the opportunity to inject a full dose of venom into Jim's leg and he foolishly ran from the ranger instead of paying the fine for early hunting. Due to his running, the venom had worked its way throughout Jim's bloodstream. As Jim sat in his rowboat, he realized that he may not live to see the next day. His entire body was on fire, his heart felt like it was being crushed in vice grips, and he was beginning to blackout. Since he was deep in the forest, there was no cell phone reception. He pulled his wallet out and lay on his back in the boat looking at the night time sky. Jim figured that the driver's license in his wallet would help the authorities identify his body. Far from being a perfect Christian, his only resolve was to make things right with his maker before dying. Jim simply said, "Lord Jesus, please forgive me." Then he blacked out. Jim woke up hours later by hearing a loud thud. Thankfully he wasn't sitting in hell or in a local jail cell. Amazingly, his boat drifted for 3 hours on the river and landed ashore. The boat landed directly next to his car! This is impossible, he thought because the way the boat was on the shoreline, it had to be pushed up there by someone. Besides that, he should have drifted miles down river, but he somehow managed to land directly next to his car. Even though his leg was swollen, his snakebite healed without going to the hospital. To this day Jim remembers the night that he apologized to God and in return God sent someone to treat his leg and to row his boat to the shoreline.

Angel on 9/11

Speaking of Angels helping us out, let me tell about my friend Mike Ryan. Officer Ryan was one of the brave police officers that were called to help evacuate people on the tragic day of September 11th, 2001. Like many other officers, Mike risked his life to help people on the day of the terrorist attack. When the buildings fell, many people were overcome by the amount of smoke and dust in the air, especially the police officers on the scene.

Unlike the fire department, many of the policemen had no breathing apparatus to protect their lungs. From the constant exposure to the dust and heat, many people experienced dehydration and coughing spells. At one point Mike became dehydrated and began coughing uncontrollably from the dust. A fellow officer appeared out of nowhere and gave Mike a large bottle of water. Mike quickly sipped the water and turned around to thank the officer. When he looked, the entire street was clear. Mike thought he was hallucinating, but he still had the water bottle in his hand. Mike is now retired from the police force and working in full time ministry. Mike will always quote this Bible verse regarding Angels:

Be not forgetful to entertain strangers: for thereby some have entertained angels unawares. (Hebrews 13:2)

Angelic Food Delivery

My friend Thomasene Campbell of North Carolina had her Angelic Food Drop in a different way. Back in 1987 she used to live in the Bitter Root Valley section of Montana. She describes the belief among some of the Christians of that area that eating organic foods and shopping at the health food store was New Age behavior which bordered idolatry. Undeterred, she kept her love for eating healthy, but when talk of prepping began to come up she began to ponder about the LORD providing for her. Thomasene lived by herself and didn't make much money working part time at a bakery. A woman that prays to God constantly, she decided to ask God if He would provide for her when the tough times came to America.

The next morning she went to work as usual and returned home to find the most unusual surprise. On her kitchen table she discovered that someone had left her an assortment of foods on her kitchen table. Everything on the table was the hard to find and expensive organic food that she loved. There was brown rice, whole wheat flour, vegetables, fruits, raw chicken and ice cream.

Mysteriously, the chicken was cool and the ice cream was not melted. Every single item on the table was of a high quality and it was only the exact foods that Thomasene would eat. The Holy Spirit then spoke to her and said, "Don't worry daughter, I will provide for you."

Hired Guns

When people watch Hollywood movies they associate a hired gun with an assassin or a hit man from the mafia. The same way a mobster can hire a hit man on an enemy in the natural realm, these altercations manifest in the spiritual realm too. As I was writing this book, my childhood friend Lisa called me with some shocking news. Lisa was recently involved in a legal battle with a Jamaican witch doctor's daughter. One night while sleeping, Lisa was given a vision of a secret voodoo ceremony in Jamaica. Lisa saw the witch doctor and her daughter casting spells over a tiny doll with the same hairstyle as Lisa. As they sprinkled blood on the doll and chanted different spells, Lisa saw the doll supernaturally come to life. However, when the doll came to life the witches immediately chanted, "Die, die, die!"

At that moment Lisa was back in her apartment in New York laying in her bed. As she opened her eyes and looked into the corner of her bed room, a huge black, eight foot demon with red eyes attacked her. As it attempted to kill Lisa by strangulation, Lisa screamed, "The blood of Jesus!"

Immediately, someone grabbed the demon and threw it across the room. Then Angels appeared in the room with swords of fire and began hacking the demon to pieces. She said the speed in which the Angels moved was similar to lightning striking in the sky. Lisa realized that the witch doctor's daughter was trying to have her killed by demonic methods because she knew Lisa was going to win the legal battle. The witch doctor attempted to bring in an assassin from the underworld, but because Lisa knew the name of Jesus, the Angels showed up to protect her.

Dan and his daughter

By now I hope you have learned that not only can an Angel fight for you in the physical realm but they can cause havoc in the unseen realm. I have a prepper friend named Dan that feared his daughter's drug problem would take her life eventually. Like many preppers, he was also concerned her demons would try to ruin his prepping endeavors for the rest of the family. Having a drug addict around your house when a disaster happens can spell trouble for a prepper. Especially if you have valuables in your home like gold, silver, cash, and guns. Dan began to pray and fast for his daughter to be released from the demonic stronghold of drugs and alcohol. Finally, one late night he was in tears praying to God to unleash Angels to free his daughter from her addictions. It was at that moment, Dan heard the sound of swords clashing above his house. It sounded like a sword-fight from some medieval type action thriller. The next day, Dan found out that his daughter had decided to quit her drug use and accept Jesus Christ as her savior. She has been clean ever since he heard the Angelic fighting above his house!

In the Bible, there is a powerful story that illustrates the incident that occurred at Dan's home:

1In the third year of Cyrus king of Persia a thing was revealed unto Daniel, whose name was called Belteshazzar; and the thing was true, but the time appointed was long: and he understood the thing, and had understanding of the vision.

2In those days I Daniel was mourning three full weeks.

3I ate no pleasant bread, neither came flesh nor wine in my mouth, neither did I anoint myself at all, till three whole weeks were fulfilled.

4And in the four and twentieth day of the first month, as I was by the side of the great river, which is Hiddekel;

5Then I lifted up mine eyes, and looked, and behold a certain man clothed in linen, whose loins were girded with fine gold of Uphaz:

6His body also was like the beryl, and his face as the appearance of lightning, and his eyes as lamps of fire, and his arms and his feet like in colour to polished brass, and the voice of his words like the voice of a multitude.

7And I Daniel alone saw the vision: for the men that were with me saw not the vision; but a great quaking fell upon them, so that they fled to hide themselves.

8Therefore I was left alone, and saw this great vision, and there remained no strength in me: for my comeliness was turned in me into corruption, and I retained no strength.

9Yet heard I the voice of his words: and when I heard the voice of his words, then was I in a deep sleep on my face, and my face toward the ground.

10And, behold, an hand touched me, which set me upon my knees and upon the palms of my hands.

11And he said unto me, O Daniel, a man greatly beloved, understand the words that I speak unto thee, and stand upright: for unto thee am I now sent. And when he had spoken this word unto me, I stood trembling.

12Then said he unto me, Fear not, Daniel: for from the first day that thou didst set thine heart to understand, and to chasten thyself before thy God, thy words were heard, and I am come for thy words.

13But the prince of the kingdom of Persia withstood me one and twenty days: but, lo, Michael, one of the chief princes, came to help me; and I remained there with the kings of Persia.

(Daniel 10:1-13)

In the passage I referenced above, the prophet Daniel was visited by an Angel of God. The Angel explained that he was coming to aid Daniel from the first day he prayed and fasted, but he had to battle a demonic entity named the Prince of Persia before coming. Amazingly, the battle in the unseen realm lasted twenty one days! Just like Daniel, my friend Dan from South Carolina went into period of fasting and prayer to break the demonic stronghold off of his beloved daughter. A key for preppers to walk away with is to be ready to combine prayer and fasting for Angelic assistance.

Chew on this for a moment. If one Angel can take out 185,000 men, is it not logical to get a good relationship with their commander in chief? Especially where prepping is concerned, a prepper needs that extra edge. Angels take orders from God, but God can allow Angels to have more "wiggle room" if the conditions are right. Ask yourself these questions and be honest:

Are you a firm believer in Jesus Christ?
Do you pray and fast often?
Have you removed sinful behavior from your life?
Have you forgiven people that have offended you?
Do you bless the poor when opportunity arises?
Do you tithe? (Give a tenth of your money, resources, or time to Christ centered churches or charities.)

I ask these questions because the Bible says in James 5:16 that "the prayers of a righteous man availeth much". If that is the case, I think we all should develop a close personal relationship with Jesus Christ. How serious do you think I am? Let me illustrate my point. Recently, I lost my Ipod mp3 player. I checked everywhere for two months straight. It really annoyed me because I would use it to listen to Christian podcasts from around the world as well as great motivational speakers. One day I got fed up because I did not want to buy another Ipod neither did I want to go the gym without something to listen to. I prayed this prayer in the morning, "Father, I do not want to waste the money you give me. If it's in your will, please have one of your Angels return my Ipod to me in Jesus name I pray, amen." That afternoon I was out in the front yard unloading my delivery van when I heard God say to my inner voice, "Start worshipping me." I put down the packages and began shouting Hallelujah and Praise the Lord! I only did if for about 3 minutes, but I was loud and intense (like any other former southern Baptist). I didn't know why God wanted me to do that but I figured it was best to be obedient. I ran in the house to grab something from my desk and my heart nearly stopped. My Ipod sat on the desk directly next to my keyboard! A miracle to say the least because I was home alone and I use my computer desk every day.

(Key bible verses about angels, 1 Peter 3:22 / Hebrews 1:14 / Psalm 104:4 / Psalm 91:11)

To my prepper friends reading this, suppose you lose the keys to your car while walking through the woods? What if you lose your fire starter, your cell phone, or even your bug out bag? If you are a believer in Jesus Christ, you have the authority in you to ask God to send an Angel to return your lost item. Humans don't realize that God has hundreds of thousands of Angels at His disposal, but they are not permitted to move unless they are given an assignment. Ask God to keep an Angel around you, your family, and your property. If we as preppers can focus on the things of God, and not our guns, the results will be fantastic.

Remember these reasons why an Angel is superior to the AR-15:

- Both are battle tested but only one has stood the test of time.
- An AR-15 can jam but Angels will get you out of a jam.
- The AR-15 rifle is accurate depending on weather conditions but Angels are accurate in any kind of weather.
- The AR-15 can only engage a limited number of targets on the battlefield, yet an Angel can engage anything on a

battlefield. Including but not limited to tanks, planes, and drones.
- Gun control laws can stop you from having any rifle including an AR-15. Man made laws can not stop God from sending armed Angels.
- An AR-15 will not help you if you encounter a demon, a grizzly bear, or even a Satanic fallen angel / alien. Angels on the other hand can defeat them in milliseconds.

For I will not trust in my bow, neither shall my sword save me.
(Psalm 44:6)

Sources
He Came to Set the Captives Free, by Rebecca Brown, MD p. 56-57
**Angels: God's Secret Agents*, by Billy Graham p. 5

Author's Note: A sinful life can stop Angelic Intervention. If you are engaging in sinful behavior, God is under no obligation to send His Angels to assist you.

Now we know that God heareth not sinners: but if any man be a worshipper of God, and doeth his will, him he heareth. (John 9:31)

Chapter 11

Disarmament

Do you think this was my desire to make this my most controversial chapter? Not at all, but it does need to be discussed when topics of such as religion, social chaos, and emergency preparedness are discussed. I will first like to say that guns are nothing more than the sword of the day. A human being can take any abstract object and use it for good or for evil. I can go to my local hardware store and purchase a few bags of fertilizer to grow a massive sized garden to feed the people within my community or I can take those same bags of fertilizer to create a bomb to terrorize an entire nation. (By the way, we have not banned fertilizer.) A box cutter can be used by a warehouse employee to unpack hundreds of deliveries at his local supermarket or it can be used by terrorist to hijack airplanes in New York City. (By the way, we have not banned box cutters.)

Being a black pastor and a black prepper, I have encountered some of the weirdest ideologies when it comes to the topic of owning a firearm. I have heard some people say, "Christians should not carry guns".

I reply to them, "Have you ever been to a church service in Pakistan, Egypt, Nigeria or Iraq?"

The answer is usually "no".

I notice this question normally comes from Christians from the United States, Canada and England. Since they have not faced religious persecution on the scale of biblical times, they enjoy a false sense of security. I inform them that in many areas around the world, armed security guards are literally inside the church meetings. These people literally risk their lives just by becoming a

Christian. As they sit peacefully in their meeting, a masked gunman sometimes will come inside and open fire with a machine gun or simply drop off a time bomb.

Some of these Christians will still try to argue with me about owning a firearm and then I have to name drop a few biblical characters on them with a modern day urban twist. If these famous men from the Bible lived today, we may describe them like this:

King David- A farmer, modern day sniper, and war hero. Later became president and private gun owner. He also co-wrote the book of Psalms in his quiet time. Ironically, this is the most read book by military men around the world.

King Solomon- In today's society we would call Solomon a lover and not a fighter, yet he pulled a machine gun and threatened to cut a child in half during a major court case when the defendant was lying under oath. In today's terms, he used a gun as a lie detector.

Samuel- The holy man became God's one man firing squad since King Saul didn't have the guts to kill the hybrid King Agag. The Bible says "Samuel hewn Agag to pieces."

Nehemiah- A holy man that rebuilt Jerusalem with a construction crew armed with AK 47s. They were on 24 hour watch for terrorism.

Simon Peter- He was Jesus Christ's disciple as well as personal armed bodyguard for 3 and a half years. He had to carry a gun when carrying around large amounts of cash from his fishing business.

Cornelius the Centurion- High ranking military leader with great morals. Always had at least 100 soldiers with guns under his control. He became good friends with Jesus when his servant was healed of cancer.

A deeper look at disarmament

Let's look at the definition of **disarmament** to bring deeper thought to this chapter. According to most dictionaries, the word disarmament is the reduction or withdrawal of military forces and weapons. Did you know there are two ways to **disarm** a human being? You can do it physically and spiritually.

You, the reader may be wondering; how does one get disarmed spiritually? Before I explain, let's take a look at the majestic lion. Lions are nicknamed the "King" of the jungle for many reasons. They have the perfect mix of size, strength, and agility. They will keep their pride together like we humans do, but do not hesitate to do things alone. They prefer to eat fresh food, and they have the ability to consider most animals in the jungle as an entrée. When most large animals encounter their razor sharp teeth and claws, it is normally shredded into morsels for the lion's small throat. (Just ask the water buffalo!)

However, have you ever noticed a lion that has been in a zoo or a circus? After years of captivity, the lion can become as docile as an everyday house cat. Go to the circus to see this amazing transformation. The ring leader of the circus may be a tiny man weighing 150 pounds, yet he is forcing this 600 pound dangerous animal to jump through hula hoops. To further insult the "King" of the jungle, the ring leader will sometimes have unchained lions sitting like dogs while he entertains the crowd with his display of bravery. Is the lion truly afraid of the tiny whip the ring leader wields or is it something else?

The answer is that the lion has a broken spirit. The greatest land predator has been **disarmed** spiritually. Through years of starvation, enslavement, and abuse, the animal has forgotten that he was once man's most feared creature in the wilderness. The lion has forgotten that man used to fear hunting lions for fear of retribution from the rest of the pride. The once mighty roar of the lion could be heard five miles away, but in captivity it becomes a simple growl. Simply because the lion has allowed its overseer to take away everything that makes it a lion.

Have you noticed the results of societies that attempt to move all Godly influence and behavior from the lives of the people? Since I am born in the United States of America, I will critique my own land rather than focus on a place like North Korea. The United States of America is a country founded on Judeo-Christian values. The truth of this reverberates in the writing of the constitution as well as the legal system for which many of the laws apply. Anyone who says that this isn't true is merely uninformed, a stone faced liar, or deliberately ignorant. As a young child, I attended public school in both the states of New York as well as Florida. Even though both places were polar opposites to each other they both proudly held the biblical Ten Commandments on display for the young children to read as they entered the school grounds. I do not recall any of the schools forcing us to read the plaques, but it was always there for a young child to read and to ask his teacher or fellow classmates about their meanings. Simple instructions for life such as "Thou shalt not kill" were once the norm for school children across the United States. So then what happened? We let our children become **disarmed** spiritually. I personally believe there has been a snowball effect since the court ruled to remove the Ten Commandments from public school property. The violence within the schools of America's youth is increasing.*

Multiply this with recent U.S. legislation for no prayer allowed in schools, no preaching in public, and no mentioning of even the generic name "God", the spiritual disarming of a country is completed. Communism and socialism attempt to eradicate the presence of God from their cultures. However, the problems begin with the people that do not believe the lies. Most human beings believe in a higher power, intelligent design, or a Creator. When humans are being forcefully told that their government is God, it does not sit well in the subconscious. Human beings eventually rebel to this conditioning by peaceful protest or violence. The governing authorities begin to fear losing power, so their normal reaction is usually irrational behavior. They respond with heavy handed force to maintain order among the populace.

The 1989 Tiananmen Square massacre in China is an example of spiritual and physical disarmament. Prior to the incident, the Chinese government had purged the Bible from its land with communist ideals led by Chairman Mao. In addition to controlling the minds of the people, the communist government physically disarmed their people. Ironically, the 1989 massive student movement began a protest for some of very ideals found in the Bible; God given ideals such as human rights, freedom of speech, and economic reform. The ruling elite came down with a heavy hand and thousands of people were murdered by their own government because they had no means to defend themselves.

In the United States, the movements by certain politicians to disarm the American public are quite disturbing to say the least. A politician may say they support gun rights for law abiding citizens but their actions must match their words. These are the same politicians that will sign treaties with the United Nations to remove small arms from the populace from their respective countries.** I am convinced that many politicians and tyrants read from the same playbook. Disarming a populace physically is a time tested approach to seizing absolute power. The Bible actually records an example of this:

19Now there was no smith found throughout all the land of Israel: for the Philistines said, Lest the Hebrews make them swords or spears:
20But all the Israelites went down to the Philistines, to sharpen every man his share, and his coulter, and his axe, and his mattock.
(1 Samuel 13:19-20)

To give you a brief background on this event roughly 3000 years ago, the Philistines and Israel were two warring nations. Through the constant battles, it was known for the winner to declare the governmental policies for the area. Since the Philistines had been victor of a previous battle, they made a law banning the Israelites from owning swords or spears. Thus enabling the Philistines to conduct random raids on Israel's cattle, produce, etc. Jesus Christ said something profound roughly 1000 years later pertaining to this topic:

No man can enter into a strong man's house, and spoil his goods, except he will first bind the strong man; and then he will spoil his house.
(Mark 3:27)

Again, we have the same premise as the situation I previously mentioned regarding the Philistines. If a person or government entity has malicious intent when they come to your place of abode, they will disarm you first. It is a tried and true method of tyrants, dictators, and invading armies. Remember the door to door inspections we saw in Iraq conducted by U.S. military? They were systematically disarming the populace. It is my contention that certain political interests would like that done in the United States. However, to accomplish such a task, it must be done by the stroke of a pen.

Armed and Dangerous

Recently an Atlanta housewife was home when a violent ex-convict broke into her home to burglarize in broad daylight. She immediately hid herself in the closet with her child. While in the closet she **armed herself** with her husband's pistol. The burglar attempted to pull her out of the closet and she used her husband's gun to shoot the criminal. The community and the police department applauded the woman's heroic efforts to protect her home and her child. She had every right to use lethal force and any politician or pastor that tells you different is simply delusional.***

Now let's just suppose the lady in question was an atheist and an anti-gun mom that believes a politician's motives for gun control are truly altruistic. This imaginary person would be disarmed spiritually and physically. What would be the results in the same situation? The first thing that would happen is that she would hide in her closet and attempt to call 911. The operator would tell her help is on the way. While she is waiting for help, the criminal would rob the home of her personal belongings. Instead of praying to God for help, she would fearfully hope for the best. Since she believes that guns are evil, she will reach for her trusty flashlight to defend herself. When the criminal discovers that she is in the closet, he may attempt to kill her for fear of a witness or perhaps rape her. Either way the results would be disastrous. Before the battle started, this woman was defeated because she was disarmed spiritually and physically. Since she is an atheist, she will have no spiritual power. She will have no authority to ask God to send an angel to protect her loved ones and her home. In this situation, the choice to be physically disarmed proved itself disastrous. If the criminal had heard the universal sound of a shotgun pump going "click, clack", he may have decided to run for his life without the firing of the weapon.

Let me say that I abhor robbery and rape, and I am not trying to make light of these situations because it can happen to anyone of any background and belief system. However, I feel that as certain countries descend into social anarchy, teaching preppers how to arm themselves spiritually and physically will be a crucial element of survival. Hopefully this book will be one of your tools to help you arm yourself spiritually. Now is not the time to be disarmed!

Sources

*http://www.usnews.com/news/articles/2014/06/10/incidents-of-school-crime-and-violence-on-the-rise-for-students-and-teachers
**http://www.foxnews.com/politics/2013/09/25/kerry-signs-un-arms-treaty-senators-threaten-to-block-it/
***http://www.ajc.com/news/news/local/mother-of-two-surprises-burglar-with-five-gunshots/nTnGR/

Author's note: The reason I highlighted the word **disarm** is to teach you the subtle approach of subliminal programming. Be careful of the mainstream media outlets you watch for news and entertainment, especially in the United States. Aside from faulty news reporting, there has been a carefully planned agenda using media to demonize law abiding gun owners by using incorrect terms such as "assault rifle" or "automatic machine guns".

Chapter 12

Racism Or Reality?

Controversial chapter? I prefer the term "thought provoking" instead. How much can a person's perception of race play into their decisions when it comes to being a prepper? Quite a bit. In some cases it can make someone outright ignorant.

In the fictional novel **Lights Out***, the author David Crawford skillfully displays the racist attitudes of some members of the preparedness community. In this highly recommended book on EMP disasters, the lead character Mark is asked to join a preparedness community by a wealthy ranch owner when the electric grid in the United States is shut down. Since the ranch owner was also head of operations for the preparedness community, he invited only Caucasians to live on his ranch prompting the open minded Mark to question the man's true motives and racial ideology. Needless to say, the ranch was overrun quickly by villains. However, Mark remained in his multi-cultural neighborhood and decided to use the strengths of everyone in the community. The end results were a success because Mark looked beyond skin color and cultural differences. Mark knew the wisdom of working together to make it through difficult times. Even though this was a fictional story, it showed the naked underbelly of some preparedness communities that even have the audacity to claim that they are Christians. Let me give you a real life example:

One day at a gun show in Georgia, I met a gentleman who was a firm supporter of the Nazi movement. In the days of World War II he would have been called a Nazi sympathizer. During my lengthy conversation with him I learned a lot more about the Nazi's than a high school textbook could teach. I certainly agreed with him that the Nazi's had some of the best scientific minds working for their movement. Their inventions such as the V2 rocket played a pivotal role in man making it to the moon. However, our conversation began to turn sour when the subject of the Jews came up. Just by listening to him, I heard his utter disgust for people of the Jewish race spewed before my dealer table. Even though I disagreed with some of his views, he felt compelled to tell me why the Jewish people were evil and why he chooses not to deal with them. (If he only knew the amount of Jewish people I have been blessed with to call my friends.)

Despite the man's intelligence, his ignorance was indeed alarming. This customer was a prepper, though not a Christian, he was indeed a prepper. Even though he purchased many emergency products from me, he was still doing business with Jews. Many of the CEOs of the emergency companies I deal with are Jewish men and women. As a dealer, I am just a middleman to the consumer for many of these products. Since he was so passionate of his distrust of Jews, why would he buy survival products made by Jews? Perhaps he was just being woefully ignorant. I didn't bother to ask him that question because these are the types of preppers that really need our prayers. These are the types of preppers that will end up in a situation where their racial bigotry will get exposed. Can you imagine this gentleman in a grid down situation and the hospital has been destroyed in a major disaster? What if the only doctor available is Jewish and his child is gravely ill? Will he forget the anti-Semitic nonsense or hold to his racist beliefs and risk losing the life of his child? These are questions I ponder about this man and these are the type of questions you should ask yourself about the people you may surround yourself with in the event they display a blatant racist attitude.

One night I had a prophetic dream regarding this very topic of racism in the prepper community. During the dream, I was sitting on my front porch at my home in Western North Carolina when a mini van with an African American family pulled into my driveway. The vehicle had a husband and wife, one child and the mother-in law aka Grandma. As the husband exited the car to come and talk to me I overheard Grandma in the back seat praying fervently. The husband said to me, "Please sir, can you help us? We are from Atlanta and have been driving for hours. Atlanta is under attack and our home is destroyed. Every time we stop and ask someone to help us we have been turned away. Your neighbors turned us away too, but the last one told us to come to this house. I think he told us to come here because you're also black." I was displeased when I heard the man say this because my neighbors are supposed to be Christians. A follower of Jesus Christ must be willing to bless those people not of his own house. This vision showed me with clarity that even though many call themselves "Christian", it will be their behavior that will let the world know who they truly are when things get ugly in America.

Wherefore by their fruits ye shall know them.
(Matthew 7:20)

Back to my dream: I decided to help the family by taking them in and we immediately administered some bottled water for his mother-in law. She was in the back seat sweating profusely in deep prayer. They thought she was in shock but when she opened her eyes and saw me offering her some water she started thanking God. She drank some water and got out of the car and began praising God. Her words were, "Thank you Lord Jesus. I knew you would never leave us nor forsake us. I knew you'd make a way. Thank you for having this young man ready to take us in. Thank you for blessing him with the provision. Thank you Lord Jesus! Hallelujah!" Later in the dream, it turned out the husband was ex-military and the wife was a nurse. The choice for taking them in eventually became a blessing for my family as we were able to support each other in hard times.

My message to the prepper reading this is: do not let racism block your blessings both now and in the future, especially if you claim to be Christian. You have been blessed with provisions to help your family and members of your extended family. God can choose an extended family member for you that will prove to be more trustworthy than people in your own house. Do not be so quick to turn away someone from your doorstep because of skin color. That person could be the biggest blessing walking in your midst. There is another ring of truth with the dream I just mentioned. Some of my neighbors do not talk to me because of skin color. The reality is that some of them would choose to starve before asking a "n—ger" for help. That is just sad because I would love to help them if a crisis should ever occur and have the chance to show them the love of Jesus Christ.

In a radio interview, I was once asked if the customers of my preparedness business display a look of surprise when they meet me face to face. The host of the show was referring to my beautiful dark skin tone of course, and so I had to be honest about the shocked facial expressions I come across. Some of my customers are surprised when they see me! Whether it was a gun show or a prepper convention, I believe God has used me to shatter myths and stereotypes of both preppers and Holy Spirit filled Christians.

In my preparedness business, I have met preppers of every different kind. I have met white, black, brown, yellow and any other shade you can think of. Most were Christians, but there were many other faiths including Muslims, Buddhists, and atheists. If you are in a grid down situation and you pre judged someone, you as a prepper may be stopping the opportunity to align yourself with a powerful ally. If you're one of the many Christians reading this book, may I suggest you just let people see "Jesus" when they see you. When you conform to the character and behavior of Jesus Christ, I notice that people will no longer see the color of your skin, they begin to see the countenance of your spirit.

"When a man's ways please the LORD, he maketh even his enemies to be at peace with him." Proverbs 16:7

During my gun show travels throughout the south, I was blessed to meet a Christian named Mark in Knoxville, Tennessee. Through conversation, we realized the only difference we had was skin color, because our life experiences were quite similar. Over dinner that evening, I shared with him some of my wildest encounters of God supernaturally providing for me and he told me stories of the same vein. Yet, there was one story he shared with me that I found remarkable.

Mark was a chaperone on a youth trip for his church a few years ago. The bus pulled over to a rest stop to get some gas. Meanwhile, the teenagers went to get some food. While sitting by himself outside the rest area, an elderly black man with an old style colonial era suit walked up to him. Mark greeted the old man like he would greet his grandfather because he was raised to respect his elders no matter the race. When Mark greeted him, the old man said, "Why, hello to you Mark." Mark paused for a minute because he never told the old man his name. Even more confusing to Mark was that this elderly looking black man had a British accent. His suit and top hat reminded Mark of people in the 1800s.

Mark says, "How do you know my name?"

The elderly man says, "I know everything about you Mark Thompson."

The man proceeds to tell Mark everything about Mark's life. The old man knew private details that no human on earth could possibly know. Mark became aware that the elderly black man standing before him may be an angelic being.

Mark then says, "Your not from here, are you?"

The elderly black man laughingly replies, "Oh no. I am from faaaaarr away!"

They both laughed out loud.

(Important note: Up until this point, Mark told me he was literally telling every living soul about Jesus Christ. He was totally focused on telling people the "Good News".)

The elderly man proceeded to tell Mark that God is very proud of his determination to tell people about Jesus and the angels in heaven are having constant conversations concerning him. Just then the associate pastor from Mark's congregation came over to interrupt the conversation. Mark told me that the pastor was probably wondering why Mark was staying away from the group just to speak with an old black man in an out dated suit. The pastor asked Mark to introduce him to his friend. Mark politely tried to warn the pastor that he was speaking to an Angel. The pastor looked at Mark and the elderly black man as if he heard a funny joke. He must have been thinking that Angels do not show up and talk to non clergy men and they surely don't appear to be black. The angel was not amused, so he proceeded to tell the young pastor every embarrassing detail of his life. The associate pastor's face turned as red as a lobster and he remained speechless. He tucked his tail between his leg and went back to the teenagers. Mark said the pastor looked like he had seen a ghost for the rest of the day.

Preppers listen up. The day may come when you meet an actual Angel to bail you out of a hairy situation. God can send you whichever Angel He chooses. If you have a racist bone in your body, God may decide to send an Angel of a race that you have discriminated against.

If there is anything I know about God, it is that He has an awesome sense of humor. After all, wasn't it God that created laughter... and color?

Let's play a game

Suppose war broke out between the United States and another country. (Substitute United States with your country if you like.) Supplies are running low because the war has come to your land by way of bombs and foreign soldiers. People are looting and the police have decided to stay home to protect their families. Your town board has held a meeting and voted to allow one refugee per family in the town. The town board says the homeowners can pick the person they will let live with them. Out of the five hundred people taken in by your town you are left to choose between the last three people. The air raid siren begins to blast and you don't have much time to interview the three candidates. You must make a choice quickly and get back home to get in your basement quickly. Your choices are:

Lucy – Christian Missionary. She just returned from working overseas before the war broke out. Age 25 (Asian decent)

Kwame – Delivery driver. His delivery truck stalled in your town when the war broke out and the highways closed. Age 30 (African decent)

Alfred- Former Military. He was riding the train when the war broke out and walked to your town. Strict vegetarian and does not smoke. Age 55 (Caucasian)

Since you already had a preconceived notion in your head about the basics of survival, you were leaning towards the former military man. Secondly, the thoughts of having another woman in your home would drive you crazy. Your daughters are a big enough problem with their constant complaining. The only thing she would be good for is feeding the homeless and you don't need Mother Theresa right now. The black guy looks like he should be in a rap video or trying to beat the rap. As soon as the war is over, this guy will probably deliver my television to his house... permanently.

The mayor of the town suggests that you come back the next day to speak with the three candidates because he does not want you to make a rush decision. He thinks you should pray about the decision. You ignore the mayor's advice and decide to let Alfred move in. A clean cut military man gives you the better odds of survival right? Wrong. It turns out that Al was a founding member of the Satanic church's military division in the army. Your daughters get molested and by the time you realize the trickery, he has decided to steal your guns, some food and your prized Harley motorcycle. Since he knew there was no police presence, he also thought it would be nice to leave you with a bullet in your head.

Had you prayed about the decision maybe God could have guided you to take Lucy or Kwame instead. You did not choose Lucy because she was a female and you didn't choose Kwame because he was black. The mayor gladly took Kwame after an investigation because he was a skilled mechanic, a concealed carry holder, and a Pastor. The town commissioner gladly took Lucy after an investigation because she knew all the basics of nursing and water purification due to her time working as a missionary overseas. Thankfully, this is just a fictitious scenario that would never happen in the United States. After all, we are a country of civilized intelligent people that would never make assumptions pertaining to one's race or gender. Now please take a pencil and put a big red X across the last two sentences you just read. Fun game isn't it?

Source
*Lights Out by David Crawford

Chapter 13

Demons Or Depression Or Destination?

Let me start by saying that there are different causes for mental health illnesses. Doctors, psychologists, and religious figures alike would agree that the causes and symptoms may vary per person. The medical community has listed numerous causes for mental illness including but not limited to trauma, injury, nutrition, and genetic makeup.

If you have been living under a rock for the last few years, the issue of people battling depression has dominated headlines in the United States of America. There have been some horrific killings committed by people suffering depression. In some cases the murder weapon is a gun, meanwhile other times it's their bare hands. The case studies are as mysterious as the person suffering from the mental health ailment. One second they are friendly, responsible citizens, and the next day they become a cold blooded murderer.

I have noticed a common question among some preppers concerning their family member that takes a prescription medication for depression. The question normally is: What do we do when Uncle So and So cannot get his Zoloft? Or Prozac, Xanex, etc.

Their concerns hold a lot of merit, considering the harmful side effects of these drugs as well as withdrawal effects. The last thing people want to deal with in a potential survival situation is the fear of having that relative "lose it" because you overcooked their scrambled eggs.

Please do not think I am taking this subject lightly. As an author that holds a minor in psychology from a prestigious university, I believe I can comment on this issue. Furthermore, I have a personal friend incarcerated in the New York prison system due to the mental health issues he suffered from the Iraq War. It is an issue that will create debates among the preppers and non preppers because we all know someone that suffers a mental health issue like depression. I would just like the psychologist and the prepper to answer one question: Could some of these cases actually be a demonic spirit attacking the person's mind and body?

I know a deliverance minister named Bob from Tennessee. During Bob's tenure as a minister he has often visited the mental hospitals and violent state prisons. On numerous occasions Bob began receiving telephone calls from the mental health professionals regarding Bob's method of treatment of the patients / prisoners. The staff members noticed that every time Bob visited a patient, the patient regained their sanity. In fact, Bob told me personally that up to 90% of the mental patients he saw were released back to society. Bob's secret was to do what Jesus taught us to do: Cast out the demons. Bob would simply pray over these patients and command the demon to leave in Jesus name.

And these signs shall follow them that believe; In my name shall they cast out devils; they shall speak with new tongues;
(Mark 16:17)

Many of the patients Bob had seen were written off by society. Some of them required padded rooms, straight jackets, and a myriad of drugs. The staff would be in fear of being around the patient alone because they could mount a deadly attack at any given moment. However, when the healing power of God comes in their presence, every tormenting demon is forced to leave the affected person.

Our failure in western society is that we label every mental health issue as a "form" of depression. In many cases, these people are actually being tormented by an evil spirit. Medication will help the physical body but it will not cure the actual problem. Hence the reason why there is no medical cure for mental illness, only a wide variety of "treatments". The only cure is to apply the blood of Jesus Christ.

If you are a prepper with a family member suffering mental illness, I would like to suggest seeking out a Christian deliverance ministry for your loved one. If you can not find one near you, feel free to send me an email for my assistance. You do not want to be in an emergency situation with a mentally unstable person that has run out of meds. Simply because, if they are being tormented by an evil spirit, they can be a liability to your family as well as your prepping endeavors. It is much better to cure the problem by doing it the Jesus way.

(**Author's note**: *If you are strong enough spiritually, you can cast out a demon by yourself. Meaning, you may not have to take that loved one to an actual deliverance minister. Again I advise, only if you are strong enough spiritually and filled with the Holy Spirit.*)

Destinations and Demons

When our brave men and women of the United States military went to Iraq and Afghanistan to fight, they were armed with superior technology. Their M-4 rifles have a better range than the AK-47 rifle used by the enemy. The M-4 rifle could accurately hit a man in the head from 600 yards away, meanwhile the AK-47 rifle was only accurate for 300 yards. The U.S. military had laser guided bombs as well as expensive satellites to give them images of enemy positions. Due to this military superiority, some reports indicate that the casualties sustained by the people of Iraq and Afghanistan to be well over 500,000 people including civilians.

An astonishing number of innocent people as well as enemy combatants compile into those figures. However, the alarming statistic remains with the U.S. soldiers that return safely home, only to commit suicide. Even though these wars are technically "over", the rate of suicide for returning troops is alarming. Psychologists attribute this trend to the trauma they endured at war. I used to find that to be a plausible explanation until there were reports of soldiers that did not see any "action" committing suicide. Why is it that some of the men that return from these war-zones, yet having never seen "action" return home with thoughts of suicide? It's a question that I asked some of the veterans that have actually seen "action" and were not relegated to clerical duties or the like.

To peel this delicate smelling onion, I will have to refer to some Hollywood movies based on real life events. In the **Stanley Kubrick film *The Shining***, audiences were given a dose of horror based on a true story. The lead character, Jack, moves with his family to accept a job at a hotel in a remote area of Colorado. Unbeknown to the family, the hotel was built on a Native American burial ground and the family that lived in the hotel prior to them were brutally killed inside the hotel. The family begins to see ghosts and eventually the husband is possessed by one of the evil spirits.

Remember the movie called **The Amityville Horror**? The movie was based upon a true story concerning a house in Amityville, New York. A family moved into a house that was the scene of a murder-suicide. The husband that lived in the house prior to them had killed six members of his family before ending his own life. The new owners of the home decided to buy the house despite its tormented history because of the huge price reduction of the home. The new buyers of the home left the house within 28 days because they were tormented by the evil spirits that inhabited the house. The homeowners witnessed demonic possession first hand when they began doing things that were totally out of their character. Interestingly enough, the family even reported seeing cloven footprints of a giant pig on the outside of the house in the fresh snow!

Have you examined the spiritual safety of your bug out location?

Let's suppose you were going on a nice vacation and you were told the room you reserved at the 5 star hotel was the scene of 10 people being murdered; would you still take the room? Most people reading this book would decline the room. Something in your subconscious, whether you are a Christian or an atheist, would make you feel uneasy about sleeping in that hotel room. Now, how many preppers are actually taking notice of where there bug out location resides?

There are thousands of places around the world where demonic entities lay dormant to terrorize a human being. These places could be in a house, a cave, or a large swathe of land. It generally tends to be places where there is a large shedding of blood or near burial grounds. Members of the public are conditioned to believe that this stuff is for the realm of science fiction or fantasy. The truth of the matter is that para normal entities such as demons, ghosts, and evil spirits are as real as the book you are holding. The Bible is loaded with stories of people being tormented by evil spirits and demons. The good news is that when they encountered the Holy Spirit, these people recovered immediately.

26*And they arrived at the country of the Gadarenes, which is over against Galilee.*

27*And when he went forth to land, there met him out of the city a certain man, which had devils long time, and ware no clothes, neither abode in any house, but in the tombs.*

28*When he saw Jesus, he cried out, and fell down before him, and with a loud voice said, What have I to do with thee, Jesus, thou Son of God most high? I beseech thee, torment me not.*

₂₉(For he had commanded the unclean spirit to come out of the man. For oftentimes it had caught him: and he was kept bound with chains and in fetters; and he brake the bands, and was driven of the devil into the wilderness.)

₃₀And Jesus asked him, saying, What is thy name? And he said, Legion: because many devils were entered into him.

₃₁And they besought him that he would not command them to go out into the deep.

₃₂And there was there an herd of many swine feeding on the mountain: and they besought him that he would suffer them to enter into them. And he suffered them.

₃₃Then went the devils out of the man, and entered into the swine: and the herd ran violently down a steep place into the lake, and were choked.

₃₄When they that fed them saw what was done, they fled, and went and told it in the city and in the country.

₃₅Then they went out to see what was done; and came to Jesus, and found the man, out of whom the devils were departed, sitting at the feet of Jesus, clothed, and in his right mind: and they were afraid.

₃₆They also which saw it told them by what means he that was possessed of the devils was healed.

₃₇Then the whole multitude of the country of the Gadarenes round about besought him to depart from them; for they were taken with great fear: and he went up into the ship, and returned back again.

₃₈Now the man out of whom the devils were departed besought him that he might be with him: but Jesus sent him away, saying,

₃₉Return to thine own house, and shew how great things God hath done unto thee. And he went his way, and published throughout the whole city how great things Jesus had done unto him.

(Luke 8:26-39)

Obviously, we noticed that the guy mentioned in the gospel of Luke was demon possessed. But how many people took notice of the man's surroundings? In verse 27 we are told that he did not abode in a house, but in the tombs. I argue that the conditions for demonic possession were met because he lived in the graveyard. Please keep in mind that the burial traditions of Israel during that time did not require the blood to be drained from the dead body before burial. So that entire area for the tombs had blood spilled on the earth. Another key point for modern day prepper's to notice is that he was living off the grid. It said in verse 34 that they (herdsmen) went and told it into the city. Please keep in mind that the other gospel (Mark 5:13) mentions that there were 2000 swine present during this event. One can deduce that a large swathe of acreage was needed to raise that many animals and the people of that time liked to keep burial grounds far away from their homes for fear of the undead as well as the unpleasant odor. My point is even though he was already off the grid he was still susceptible to being attacked by evil spirits, partly because of his choice of residence. Lets examine this deeper because I have heard of many preppers choosing abandoned cemeteries and haunted houses as their bug out location.

The regions of Iraq and Afghanistan have seen so much bloodshed throughout history, that there is an unparalleled level of paranormal activity within their regions. Modern day Iraq was known as Babylon in the ancient world. Both Iraq and the region known as Afghanistan have had literally millions of people die in battles by the hands of the most brutal men to walk the face of the earth. People such as Alexander the Great, Ghengis Khan, Nimrod and Saddam Hussein to name a few. If you were able to see the millions of dead bodies of the people killed in these places over the past 4000 years, you would not want to visit such a place.

How does this affect our soldiers? Many of the men and women sent to these places by the U.S. military are unaware they are stepping into this hotbed of paranormal activity. Millions of the men that died in these two regions from centuries old conflicts have never been buried. Their blood has literally touched the soil in these places. In the book of Genesis, Cain murdered his brother in a jealous rage. When God questions Cain about the crime, we need to take notice of the words God used in verse 10.

And he said, What hast thou done? the voice of thy brother's blood crieth unto me from the ground.
(Genesis 4:10)

Even though Abel was dead, his blood was very much alive. God did not need a special forensic light to see or hear the splatter of Cain's blood. In the Bible, God constantly admonishes His people to never drink blood, because there is "life in the blood." The shedding of blood upon a geographical area is not as simple as dropping a glass of water. There are profound spiritual implications when it happens, especially to innocent people. If people or preppers decide to build a house on land that has been defiled, it can spell big trouble for them in the future.

So ye shall not pollute the land wherein ye are: for blood it defileth the land: and the land cannot be cleansed of the blood that is shed therein, but by the blood of him that shed it. (Numbers 35:33)

If you read the above verse, hopefully you may get some revelation of what I am trying to explain. If you had an invading army lead a coalition into a certain area of land and many innocent people are killed, the blood or shall I say life force remains on the land, until it is cleaned by the one who did the killing or they are killed over the same geographical area of land for an atonement. Has that happened over the geographical areas I mentioned earlier? I am afraid not. But notice these key words when God is giving instruction to the children of Israel regarding blood being shed:

13And whatsoever man there be of the children of Israel, or of the strangers that sojourn among you, which hunteth and catcheth any beast or fowl that may be eaten; he shall even pour out the blood thereof, and cover it with dust.

14For it is the life of all flesh; the blood of it is for the life thereof: therefore I said unto the children of Israel, Ye shall eat the blood of no manner of flesh: for the life of all flesh is the blood thereof: whosoever eateth it shall be cut off.
(Leviticus 17:13-14)

This is where it gets deep. Scholars argue that in verse 13, God was teaching good hygiene to bury/cover the blood of dead animals with dust. Even though they are correct, I believe there is a deeper reasoning with covering the blood with dust. Whenever we see footage of a voodoo ceremony or read about some Satanic cult, the common theme is for them to drink blood to get power. In verse 14 God says ,"the blood of it is for the life thereof". Well if the blood is the life, should we have a clear understanding of what the Hebrew / Aramaic meaning of the word life when used in this context? The word for life is translated to the Hebrew word NEPHESH.

NEPHESH means soul, living being or life.

So, now do you understand why a haunted house is more than just a house where some people got killed? Are you beginning to understand that an old cemetery is more than just a place where some dead guys were buried a hundred years ago? You are actually stepping on living beings, even when you cannot see them. Is what I am saying biblical?

²⁰ And Elisha died, and they buried him. And the bands of the Moabites invaded the land at the coming in of the year.

²¹ And it came to pass, as they were burying a man, that, behold, they spied a band of men; and they cast the man into the sepulchre of Elisha: and when the man was let down, and touched the bones of Elisha, he revived, and stood up on his feet.

(2 Kings 13:20-21)

Traditional bible scholars normally will not debate God raising people from the dead by using His prophets. The prophet will normally speak over the body, breath into the body, or deliberately rub against the body for the supernatural resurrection to take place. Yet, this is the only place recorded in the Bible that a dead man came back to life simply because his corpse was dropped on top of the bones of another dead man. The word **bones** here is commonly translated into the word **substance** which is derived from the Greek word **ETSUM** which means body or life! Elisha was dead, however his blood drained back into the earth at this very location. Since Elisha was a holy prophet, could it be logical to surmise that the holy anointing that followed him in the living realm still remained on the actual ground where his corpse lay? This mystery of burial grounds will continue to cause debate for years to come, but one thing is certain, there is more happening in the unseen realm than we can truly fathom. My point is that we all need to be careful as to where we lay our heads at night, even in bug out locations. Your bug out location should be a place that is clean naturally as well as spiritually.

If you are prepper and you feel like your home or bug out location is haunted, there is hope. The solutions work really well for the followers of Jesus Christ. If you are an atheist, call one of your

Christian friends to help. Jesus said that He "gives us all power over the enemy." This includes evil spirits that may be haunting your home or bug out location.

1) Prayer walk the area- Recently, I was speaking with an elderly lady about the paranormal activity at her house. The poor lady was at her wits end because she didn't know who to tell for fear of people thinking she was crazy. She told me of things moving around the house at night as well loud sounds manifesting. I asked her for her address and decided to swing by. Without walking one step into the house, I simply walked around the house three times and prayed to God and commanded every evil spirit to leave that house in Jesus name. There was a few other prayers I said but for the sake of time I will leave them out of this story. Three months passed by and I saw the old lady at a local church. She happily told me that there hasn't been any more disturbances at night and she now sleeps like a baby. As a believer in Jesus Christ, the places your feet touch enable you to take that territory from enemies of God, and this includes unclean spirits. (Joshua 1:3, Deuteronomy 11:24)
2) I mentioned earlier that when blood is shed on the land, there should be an atonement made. For a believer in Jesus Christ, this process is quite simple and it will not require you actually getting an animal to make a sacrifice over the land or the shedding of blood of the perpetrators of crime. According to the Bible, the blood which Jesus Christ shed is the propitiation (atonement) for our sins. (1John 2:2 and Romans 3:25) If you mention this when praying over certain territories the demonic entities or evil spirits will generally pack up their bags and leave.
3) Get a certified deliverance minister or pastor to come visit the place. When I say certified I do not mean educational degrees, I am referring to a Bible believing man or woman of God that actually "hears from God". In some circles they are known as "holy spirit" filled Christians. These are the folks

that have a reputation of walking in the supernatural. There are quite a few still in church pulpits in America, however they are getting harder to find. If you do not think you are strong enough spiritually, simply pray to God to help you find the right person to come and God will send the right person.

Hopefully, I shed some light on the topics of demons, depression, and destinations. It is my hope that you use wisdom in securing the property for your new home or in the choice you make for a bug out location. I will leave you a list of places that I would use extreme caution in deciding to have as a bug out location or home site.

Site of a murder(s)
Cemetery or Crematorium Grounds
Native American Burial Grounds / Mounds
Former Plantation homes that tortured / killed African slaves
Abandoned and current Mental Homes/Institutions
Abandoned and current abortion clinics
Abandoned Prison Facilities
Animal Slaughterhouse (current and former)

Authors Note:
If you are going to use the Bible to cast away demons from a person or a property, I highly recommend the King James Bible due to the fact that demons actually know which versions of the Bible have more power. Over the years, I have heard numerous reports of people attempting to cast away a demonic presence from a person or a residence and the demon would always laugh when a person attempted to do this activity with a grammatically edited version of the Bible. For example: If you were in England and stood outside Buckingham Palace and some guy in a red coat walks up to you while smoking a marijuana joint and says, "My old lady wants to talk to you". You would ask questions pertaining to who is the lady and you may even ask the guy for credentials considering the way

he presented himself to you. If you lived in Miami for any part of your life you may even assume that this man is a pimp. Now if the same gentleman in the red coat walked up to you with his head held high without a marijuana joint and said to you, "I am her majesty's royal guard. Her majesty Queen Elizabeth requests your presence immediately." Your demeanor would change and you would be on your best behavior because you know you have been summoned by royalty. You would gather your things and move immediately. The demonic world understands angelic hierarchy and commandments from a King better than you. They will not move for peasants nor will they move for words not endorsed by the King of Kings.

There will be some pastors that will disagree with me on this subject and all I can say is that they better take this argument to God almighty. As a pastor, I can tell you that it is a sad state of affairs when I meet Muslims that respect the King James Bible more than the men that claim they are of the Christian faith.

Interesting Fact: *After reading this chapter do you think it is a coincidence that the area of land used to build the United Nations building in New York City was an area of animal slaughterhouses?*

Chapter 14

Multiple Confirmations?

Intel is a shortened form of the word intelligence especially when used in regards to military applications. It can be used in regards to spying and espionage. Here is a good example of what I mean: When the U.S. military claimed that Saddam Hussein had weapons of mass destruction in his arsenal, it was "bad intel". There has not been any definitive proof of Saddam Hussein in possession of these so called weapons. However, there is proof that Christians are being systematically murdered for their beliefs by certain radical Islamic groups in certain areas of Iraq. We have videos, pictures, and even the testimony of people who have fled those areas. Due to the numerous types of documented accounts of these atrocities we can conclude that we have "good intel". So if you hear a rumor of a future event, please thoroughly check the source of your intel. I used to get rattled when I read some conspiracy on the internet only to find out later it was a hoax. In some cases I learned that the actual information I received was part of a government misinformation campaign to spread a particular agenda or to provoke a response by certain elements within society. So instead of arguing with you about the FEMA prison camps, I believe it is more important for you to know how to decipher the good intel from the bad intel while using the spiritual realm or as we Christians call it, "the spirit of truth". There are too many people prepping with bad intel.

There is a law written by Moses found in the Bible that says out of the mouth of two or three witnesses a matter is established. (Deuteronomy 19:15) This is one of the avenues our legal system uses to convict a criminal for a crime. If two people testify against you in a court room concerning a crime, consider yourself a candidate for a vacation at Alcatraz University. This is a reason why many criminals get away with murder. If there are not two solid witnesses to the crime, a defense lawyer can easily tear apart the testimony of one witness. Hence the reason why some extremely wealthy pedophiles do not see the inside walls of a prison.

Back to my point. The same rules of engagement actually work in the spiritual realm. God does not change His laws nor His word. If you awaken yourself spiritually to the things of God, you will notice the law of two or three witnesses in different aspects of life including dreams and visions. A few years ago, my spiritual mentor (Pastor John Parault) told me that the Lord told him, "My son, do you think I warned you about Russia for nothing?" It was referring to numerous prophecies John Parault heard from other prophetic men regarding a Russian surprise attack on the United States of America. At the time John shared this information with me, I began to recall some information my military friends said concerning Russia. The military men had pretty much concluded that the only reason the United States never had war with the Russians is divine intervention. As if those memories were sobering enough, let me tell you what happened in the course of three years. Please keep in mind the law which states: at the mouth of two or three witnesses a matter is established.

On November 3, 2010 the Federal Reserve announced the next round of quantitative easing to stimulate the economy of the United States of America. Economists warned that this action may anger the Peoples Republic of China as well as the Russian Federation because of the adverse effect the money printing scheme may have on their respective economies. *

Nevertheless, the action was taken and everything seemed fine diplomatically until November 8, 2010. A missile was shot from an unidentified submarine into the sky off the coast of Southern California. The United States Navy was not conducting any tests near the area and they were "clueless" as to who would test fire a potential weapon of mass destruction. **

During the summer of 2010, there was a mysterious young man named Adam that walked to different churches throughout North Georgia and Western North Carolina warning different congregations to "begin storing medical supplies, clothing and food for our brothers coming from the Atlanta area." Most of the church leaders ignored him, but a few did listen.

One evening I had a vision that nearly made me wet the bed like a three year old child. I dreamed I was in a hotel room in Miami, Florida directly next to Miami International Airport watching the airplanes land on the runway. As I watched the American Airlines planes landing, I noticed something wasn't quite right with the next plane approaching the airport. (For those of you that don't know, American Airlines operates a major flight hub at the Miami International Airport.) The plane was actually a Russian made plane with the American Airlines logos painted all over the plane. The flight tower believed they were in contact with the plane as it made its decent into Miami's airspace. However, they were actually speaking to some type of fake digital voice impersonating itself to be the captain of the American Airlines airplane. The planes were all flying in the normal flight pattern of an airplane coming from the Caribbean, however these decoy planes came out of Cuba. By the time the flight controller at Miami International realized that the planes were decoys, it was too late. The Russians bombed Miami International Airport, downtown Miami, and every major communications outlet for South Florida. The panic upon the faces of the people was indescribable. Ironically, this vision occurred as I was considering moving back to Miami for a new job. Needless to say, I did not take the job.

A few days later, I went to a Christian retreat center in South Carolina to hear a few pastors teach on a few different issues. One particular pastor that I later became good friends with named Paul Backhaus told of an eerie vision the Lord had given him. He saw people walking the highways from Atlanta, Georgia into the mountains of Western North Carolina. The people left the metro

Atlanta area looking for places of refuge because Atlanta was no more. The Russians destroyed Atlanta with a nuclear weapon. Pastor Paul said he did not know when this would happen, but one day it will happen.

The very next morning, I left the retreat center and drove to Greenville, South Carolina to setup my booth for a gun show at the convention center. During the show, a local Pastor's wife came to my booth and purchased a large amount of emergency supplies and long term food packages. Since we have spoken in the past I felt led to ask her a personal question. "What did God show you?" She replied to me by saying, "It wasn't me, but it was my husband. I know my husband hears from God. My husband just received a startling vision of our naval base in Virginia Beach getting destroyed by Russian submarines in a sneak attack. The U.S. Navy will not get one shot off and this defeat will be worse than Pearl Harbor."

By this time I started to get a chill down my spine. I thought to myself, "what are the chances?" First some guy walking around to our churches warning people, then 3 years later I get the vision, then Pastor Paul receives a vision with the same subject matter, and then a Pastor in South Carolina getting the same type of vision. I knew this fit the criteria of having "3 witnesses", but I soon found out that God had revealed this same vision to numerous Christians throughout the United States. Some of these men are well known individuals in their respective ministries including Dimitri Dudamon, Dr. Henry Gruver, David Taylor, etc.

A question that arose in my natural mind was: How come the major preachers on television aren't reporting any of these divine dreams of God's judgment on the United States of America? The answer was summed up in one word: money. If they gave this warning to America: Stop sinning or God is going to allow the Russians to overthrow us just like he allowed destruction to happen to ancient Israel! I can bet their ratings will drop and so will the financial donations, but if they continue to tell people "Live your best life now!" it sounds much more pleasing to the ear.

The other reason why many clergy members in America don't mention these visions is because of fear of rejection. God will give these men and women a warning sign in the form of a prophetic dream or vision but they will choose not to tell the congregation because of fear. Many times if a member of church tells congregants of a prophetic dream given to them by God, they are sometimes called crazy and become an outcast. In some cases these churches have board members that approve the sermons of the pastor and if that pastor gets out of line, they simply cast a vote to fire their pastor. (Word to the wise: Churches are supposed to be led by the Holy Spirit, not by votes and politics.)

The Bible is filled with cases of people that get a prophetic vision from God only to be persecuted for telling everyone. Joseph was rejected by his family members for a futuristic dream he had of everyone bowing to him in the book of Genesis (37:9-10). Another blatant example of telling unpopular visions comes from the second book of Chronicles (18:8-26). The young prophet Micaiah warns Ahab the King of Israel that his military will be defeated. Micaiah is immediately thrown in prison as a result of the unpopular warning.

If you are reading this book and God had given you multiple dreams and visions regarding the future of your country, then you have a biblical mandate to give a warning. You may have the calling of a watchman and your job is to warn the people, whether they want to hear it or not. There are two passages that you should become familiar with. One of them is Ezekiel 33 verses 1 through 8. It reads:

[1] *Again the word of the LORD came unto me, saying,*

² Son of man, speak to the children of thy people, and say unto them, When I bring the sword upon a land, if the people of the land take a man of their coasts, and set him for their watchman:

³ If when he seeth the sword come upon the land, he blow the trumpet, and warn the people;

⁴ Then whosoever heareth the sound of the trumpet, and taketh not warning; if the sword come, and take him away, his blood shall be upon his own head.

⁵ He heard the sound of the trumpet, and took not warning; his blood shall be upon him. But he that taketh warning shall deliver his soul.

⁶ But if the watchman see the sword come, and blow not the trumpet, and the people be not warned; if the sword come, and take any person from among them, he is taken away in his iniquity; but his blood will I require at the watchman's hand.

⁷ So thou, O son of man, I have set thee a watchman unto the house of Israel; therefore thou shalt hear the word at my mouth, and warn them from me.

⁸ When I say unto the wicked, O wicked man, thou shalt surely die; if thou dost not speak to warn the wicked from his way, that wicked man shall die in his iniquity; but his blood will I require at thine hand.

Remember what I said about two witnesses? Here is another verse regarding the same subject matter. Written in plain English, the text reads:

"When I say unto the wicked, Thou shalt surely die; and thou givest him not warning, nor speakest to warn the wicked from his wicked way, to save his life; the same wicked man shall die in his iniquity; but his blood will I require at thine hand."

(Ezekiel 3:18)

Now let's get back to my premise. The people of the United States of America are getting "bad intel" regarding our country's relationship with Russia. The controlled media in the U.S. will say the relationship is "strained". The media gives us all kind of soft words to keep the public alarm bells from ringing. The honest truth is that U.S. / Russian relations are the worst they have been since the days of the Cuban missile crisis. News agencies around the world as well as alternative media websites are reporting the dangerous tensions between the two superpowers. If you would like to verify if what I am saying is true, I encourage you to type in "War with Russia" into your internet search engine and you will discover a litany of news sources exposing this clear and present danger.

If you can sense in your spirit that what I am writing is true, then I suggest you act on it. The most important thing you can do to prepare is to accept Jesus Christ as your personal Lord and Savior. If you are physically able, get on your knees and say "Lord Jesus, please forgive me for my sins. Come into my heart and change me. Please guide my life from this day forward. I know what this author is saying is true, so please provide a hedge of protection for me and my family. Amen"

If you are physically able, try to find yourself a small size church or Bible study that reads from the King James Bible. If you are not physically able, simply ask God to heal you of your physical problem. If you need someone to pray with you or for you, simply email me and I will try to contact you. I have too many stories of people being supernaturally healed through the power of prayer!

Do you feel an unction in your spirit to move out of the big city? Start praying about it with an urgency. There seems to be an influx of people moving out of the city into the countryside of the United States. Some of them are Christians and some of them are not, but the reality is, these people are "sensing" some type of drastic change in the near future. Hopefully, this book will also provide useful spiritual tools to your preparation efforts for the near future.

On a finishing note, a former military chaplain named Al Cuppet recently said on Omega Man internet radio interview that his friend named Bob had seen a prophetic vision of Pastors being chased and beaten by their congregations. Why? Because the church leaders didn't warn their church members of all these horrendous changes they were going to see in the United States of America! Hopefully, I won't be one of those Pastors.

Rapture or Rupture?

Since this chapter is titled Multiple Confirmations, I thought I may end it by discussing the Rapture. It is a touchy subject among Christians because many disagreements have turned into heated arguments pertaining to certain verses in the New Testament. For those of you not well versed with the Bible, it is a doctrine based on the belief that Jesus Christ will sweep up the believers to heaven right before God unleashes His wrath of judgment on the earth.

Many Christians in the Western World believe they will not endure any suffering because they will be supernaturally swept away by God. Some of these precious brothers and sisters believe that God will rapture them because they are citizens of the United States. These are primary reasons why many Christians in the United States choose not to prepare for turbulent times. Many Christians feel the "prepper" minded Christians are lacking faith, yet it is these mainstream Christians that run to the prepared Christian for aid when disaster strikes. It is quite an interesting paradox, and at times comical. The Bible clearly says that "God is a respecter of no persons", so please do not make the mistake of confusing God for a customs agent before the rapture. He will not be asking for your nationality and passport picture!

On a serious note, I believe that Jesus Christ is coming back to earth, but I also believe He will do it when He is ready, not when I am ready. In other words, God operates on His timetable, not mine or yours. The confirmation for this statement is in the history books.

The Twin Tower Attacks
Hurricane Andrew
Hurricane Katrina
The Asian Tsunami
The Fukushima Disaster
The slaughter of Christians worldwide including but not limited to:
The killing of Christians in China
The killing of Messianic Jews in Nazi Germany
The killing of Christians by Joseph Stalin
The killing of Christians by Idi Amin
The killing of Christians by Fidel Castro
The killing of Christians by ISIS militants
The killing of Christians by Al Queda

Death by natural disasters and murder of the faithful has occurred in the scenarios I listed above. I just have one question: Where was the Rapture?

Sources

*http://money.cnn.com/2010/11/03/news/economy/fed_decision/

**http://abcnews.go.com/Politics/mystery-missile-launched-missile-off-california-coast/story?id=12097155

(**Author's note**: The other confirmation is in the chapter titled Change the Weather. War and a major natural disaster is looming.)

Chapter 15

Change the weather Or Weather the Change?

Bad news! An F5 tornado is on a direct path to your homestead and the weather forecaster said to expect massive casualties. Your first thought is to get everyone in your family tucked away inside the underground storm shelter and your second thought is to make sure all of your essentials are secured. These items include food, water, cash, and ID. As you and your loved ones hunker down, your mind begins to wonder. These questions bombard your mind:

- How will the house hold up?
- Did I pay the insurance for the house and car?
- Will my farm be destroyed?
- Will my animals be killed?
- Will my preps be destroyed in seconds?

As you sit there sweating profusely in fear, the old farmer down the road is as cool as the other side of the pillow. Farmer Jack has seen plenty of tornadoes during his 70 years of living and he knew the secret to get through the storm. Old Jack did all the same preparations and he is a prepper just like you. The farmer's family gathered together to get into the storm shelter and double checked that they had all the essentials with them. However, as they closed the storm shelter's doors, the family immediately formed a circle and began to pray. They prayed for God to protect them during the storm and to put HIS hand of protection over their entire property.

The tornado ravishes the area, yet there are some weird anomalies. In one particular area the storm cut a swath of destruction through real estate but some of the homes remained untouched. One of those homes belonged to good old Farmer Jack. Aside from no electricity, his entire property looked pretty much the same. Your property didn't fare so well. As you sort through the damage, you wonder why your property took the brunt of the storm. Luckily, you are friends with that old farmer next door. Since the farmer is a fellow prepper, you know that you will have help with the basic supplies you need until the insurance company writes the check for your damages. The prepper inside you begins to ponder: "If the grid was down, I would be really screwed because there would be no homeowners insurance to help me rebuild. There has to be a way to protect my family from these storms."

After watching a couple of episodes of **National Geographic's Doomsday Preppers**, I noticed that many preppers are concerned with possible weather and natural disasters. They share a legitimate concern of hurricanes, tornadoes, earthquakes and the like. The images of Hurricane Katrina stay in the subconscious of both preppers and regular everyday people. Even though these threats are real, perhaps its time to learn how to defeat them in the spiritual realm. Jesus demonstrated this during His ministry on earth:

^{37} *And there arose a great storm of wind, and the waves beat into the ship, so that it was now full.*

^{38} *And he was in the hinder part of the ship, asleep on a pillow: and they awake him, and say unto him, Master, carest thou not that we perish?*

^{39} *And he arose, and rebuked the wind, and said unto the sea, Peace, be still. And the wind ceased, and there was a great calm.*

^{40} *And he said unto them, Why are ye so fearful? how is it that ye have no faith?*

⁴¹ And they feared exceedingly, and said one to another, What manner of man is this, that even the wind and the sea obey him?

(Mark 4:37-41)

Can a prepper have faith to alter the weather like Jesus did?

Yes you can! If you are a prepper that believes in your heart that Jesus Christ died on the cross for your sins then anything is possible. Obviously, God has the last say in these types of requests but you should be aware of the possibilities. Jesus said a truly profound statement for the people that will believe in him. In the gospel of John he said, "Truly, truly, I say to you, he who believes in Me, the works that I do, he will do also; and greater works than these he will do…" (John 14:12)

One day I was doing some outdoor work for a subdivision in the mountains of North Carolina. Like most of these jobs you can not pick up your pay until you are finished with the job. This particular job included mowing, weed eating and tree limbs to be cut. Upon nearing completion, a thunderstorm began to roll in. The dark clouds rolled in quickly with a few lightning bolts to boot. I needed about another hour to finish the job that day because I was heading out of town for business. If I didn't get paid that day, it would cause financial problems for my planning. I sat in my van and watched as the torrential down pour began. Suddenly, I grew the courage to pray to ask God keep the area I was trimming dry until I finished. I then walked outside the van into the heavy rain and yelled, "I rebuke you in Jesus name! Rain wait until I am finished!" I went back into the van and pulled out the weed trimmer and began to cut the weeds in defiance. The rain began to dramatically slowdown to a light summer mist. It was perfect weather to work in because the mist kept you cool in the humid weather. It wasn't until a few minutes later that I noticed the magnitude of the miracle because my music headphones were drowning out the background noise. The violent rain storm was still ongoing around the entire mountain I was working on! As I looked in the distance of about 100 yards, there was a wall of rain water surrounding the entire area I was working. Literally at the moment I finished my trimming an hour later, the rain storm took dominion of the area I just completed.

As a prepper, I understand that weather can be a factor that can ruin a self sufficient lifestyle. Bad weather can ruin the plans of people anywhere on the planet, however a prepper that possesses the knowledge of the authority that Christ has given them will not have to accept the outcome of an unbeliever. There are numerous stories of people that believed that God would hear them when they prayed in unison for a change in weather and it occurred. Back in 1999, my brother died in a car accident. Since the funeral was being held in Miami during hurricane season, my family grew nervous of the hurricane that was fast approaching Miami the very weekend of the funeral services. Family and friends from all over the world were flying in to pay their last respects to a Christian missionary that had impacted hundreds of lives. The weather satellite showed the hurricane on a direct path for Miami and airlines were beginning to cancel flights. My family and friends all began to pray in unison for God to move the hurricane so people could come to Miami and leave Miami safely. Within one day the hurricane changed direction and headed north. The funeral services happened without any stoppages and about 300 people accepted Jesus Christ as their savior!

Bad Weather Blessing?

I learned that weekend that miracles happen much easier if your will lines up with God's will. I don't think God was going to lose sleep if my brother's funeral was cancelled, but God takes a serious interest in people hearing about Jesus Christ. All that was required was people to have faith to pray together in unison for the hurricane to move from its path. Preppers should understand that God does not like human beings killing each other and He especially does not like it when believers in His son Jesus Christ engage in that activity. So in the future, why not try focusing your prayers in a different direction when the trouble comes? If society falls apart tomorrow and there are some unsavory characters roaming your neighborhood, up to no good, perhaps this is a prayer that you should use:

"My father in heaven: There are some evil men looking to harm my family. If it is your will for me to not kill anyone, please send all manners of bad weather to blind and confuse their path. In Jesus name we pray; amen."

There are cases when bad weather may arise and the situation becomes a blessing. My friend David from England witnessed this while in a pretty dicey situation. Years ago, David was one of the Christians that smuggled Bibles into the former Soviet Union. The atheist government could punish anyone with a Bible with jail time, beatings, seizure of goods and even death. A foreign citizen charged with this offense could sometimes be found in an unmarked grave. During a Bible smuggling trip in Russia, David had to meet his contact at a campground. Even though the place was packed with hikers and vacationers, the secret police were still nearby. Sensing he was being watched, David grew nervous of the massive pile of Bibles in his camper. When he met up with his contact to drop off the Bibles, the contact confirmed David's suspicions. They were being watched by someone from the secret police. The duo knew they had to ditch the Bibles quickly. They prayed for God to make a way for the Bibles to be distributed among the Russian people without them getting caught. Just then a hiking club consisting mainly of young college students with their own tents and campers rolled into the park. There were so many of them arriving that the campground looked like a Woodstock concert. On this bright beautiful day a sudden rain cloud appeared. As if someone hit a light switch, the park became dark grey and buckets of rain came down. The visibility in the park was reduced to near zero. David and his contact knew that this was a divine act of God considering there was a zero percent chance of rain in the weather report. Under the cover of the blistering rain, they distributed the Bibles to some of the college students who then distributed the boxes to friends in the campers and tents. The college students knew they could easily argue to the authorities that the Bible books are part of their college studies. As soon as David and his partner were finished unloading the illegal contraband, the sun came back out. The secret police did not see anything worth reporting. After David left the park and drove miles away he was detained by the secret police, but they didn't find any Bibles on him. They just found a tourist in wet clothing from the "freak" rainstorm.

And it came to pass, as they fled from before Israel, and were in the going down to Bethhoron, that the LORD cast down great stones from heaven upon them unto Azekah, and they died: they were more which died with hailstones than they whom the children of Israel slew with the sword.
(Joshua 10:11)

Federal Fog

On the night of August 29, 1776 General George Washington had to evacuate his men from Long Island to New York. The British Army and their 30,000 men had blocked the roads leaving the only way of escape for Washington's 8,000 men by sea. Washington's men had only rowboats at their disposal and the British Army had massive battle ships at theirs. If the British discovered their route of escape, his men could easily be killed. It was at this juncture where George Washington prayed to God for a miracle. Facing certain death, his men climbed in their rowboats in the early morning hours. As the massive evacuation took place, the men feared the rising sun revealing their escape. Then the miracle which changed the direction of the war occurred. A massive fog bank rolled into the entire area. Some witnesses indicated that visibility was less than six yards. The British did not realize the escape until the mysterious fog had passed. George Washington and his men were able to regroup and fight the British another day, paving the way for George Washington to become the President of the United States.*

Demonic Weather?

God is not the author of all bad weather on the planet. There are some cases when the weather is actually sent from the devil himself. Preppers need to identify if the weather is a God induced weather pattern or if there is a demonic element attached to the change in climate. Proof of demonic activity in the weather is proven in the Bible when God gives Satan permission to put Job through a harsh test:

12And the LORD said unto Satan, Behold, all that he hath is in thy power; only upon himself put not forth thine hand. So Satan went forth from the presence of the LORD.
13And there was a day when his sons and his daughters were eating and drinking wine in their eldest brother's house:
14And there came a messenger unto Job, and said, The oxen were plowing, and the asses feeding beside them:
15And the Sabeans fell upon them, and took them away; yea, they have slain the servants with the edge of the sword; and I only am escaped alone to tell thee.
16While he was yet speaking, there came also another, and said, The fire of God is fallen from heaven, and hath burned up the sheep, and the servants, and consumed them; and I only am escaped alone to tell thee.
17While he was yet speaking, there came also another, and said, The Chaldeans made out three bands, and fell upon the camels, and have carried them away, yea, and slain the servants with the edge of the sword; and I only am escaped alone to tell thee.
18While he was yet speaking, there came also another, and said, Thy sons and thy daughters were eating and drinking wine in their eldest brother's house:

19And, behold, there came a great wind from the wilderness, and smote the four corners of the house, and it fell upon the young men, and they are dead; and I only am escaped alone to tell thee.

Most scholars agree that the fire of God falling from heaven is a reference to being struck by lightning back in verse 16. However if you take careful notice of verse 19, we read that a "great wind" came from the wilderness to topple the house. The leader of the demonic world actually used bad weather to kill the family members of Job. When God gave Satan permission to harm Job in verse 12, Satan was explicitly told that he is not allowed to lay his hands on Job, but using bad weather to kill his family seemed to be on the option board.

Is that too much for you to swallow because of Grandma's religion? During a naval war, it is commonly understood that if the General of the opposing army is on a battleship, the opposite force would try their best to sink that ship. Well, what do you think Satan was doing back in the book of Mark? He was trying to drown Jesus and his lieutenants at sea. Jesus knew the storm was a demonic attack, hence the reason why He rebuked the storm the same way He rebuked demons from sick people. If you're a prepper with the true intentions of helping people with your supplies in the event of serious disaster, then learn to fight demonic weather conditions with the same authority that Jesus showed us two thousand years ago!

Tsunami of Change

Many times in biblical history God has been known to use natural disasters as a method of judgment upon a nation or a signal of warning. The worldwide flood that occurred during Noah's day would be considered a judgment. The hail that fell on the Egyptians during the days of Moses could be considered a warning because Pharaoh had a chance to release the Israelites to avoid further plagues. The three and a half year rain drought that occurred during

Elijah's ministry was a judgment for the wickedness of Israel's leadership. However, there is one highly debated weather anomaly that occurred in Sodom and Gomorrah. The ancient text reads:

²⁴ Then the LORD rained upon Sodom and upon Gomorrah brimstone and fire from the LORD out of heaven;

²⁵ And he overthrew those cities, and all the plain, and all the inhabitants of the cities, and that which grew upon the ground.

There are a few researchers of both biblical and non-biblical backgrounds that have theorized that these events were done by small meteorites hitting the earth or fragments of a comet. I find the theories highly interesting because they point out the possible scientific outcomes in this scenario. If you are interested in learning more about how comets and meteors play a role in history and Bible prophecy, I recommend you visit the website **www.thecometsofgod.com** featuring the work of **Dr. Jeffrey Goodman**.

Here is my point: There is a prophecy concerning a tsunami hitting the Eastern United States, but the cause of it will not be a traditional earthquake. The cause of it will be from meteorites landing in the ocean. The chances of this happening is probably like winning the lotto: twice. I mean the chances are so slim it would be like winning the lottery two different times, with two different debit cards used at two different stores. So if this does happen, the insurance companies will claim an indemnity because it is an act of God. That is exactly the nature of God. Whether it is Moses parting the Red Sea, Jesus returning from the dead, or the blind receiving their sight; God likes to make sure He gets the credit for impossible events taking place.

For mine own sake, even for mine own sake, will I do it: for how should my name be polluted? and I will not give my glory unto another.

(Isaiah 48:11)

Let me express what God is saying in the modern hip hop vernacular: "You simpletons on earth will not get the credit for the things that I do." Of course, human beings try their best to do it anyway with the end result of looking like an educated fool. If this tsunami pulverizes the Eastern United States, the results may be apocalyptic because of the amount of nuclear power plants along the east coast. The nuclear reactor damage after the Fukishima earthquake in Japan will pale in comparison to the devastation faced in the United States if a massive tsunami hits the Eastern United States. Do you recognize any of the following names:

Salem and Hope Creek Nuclear Station – New Jersey
Saint Lucie Plant-Florida
Brunswick Steam Electric Plant-South Carolina
Pilgrim Nuclear Power Station-Massachusetts
Millstone Power Station – Connecticut

These are just a few of the nuclear power stations that lie along the east coast of the United States. An interesting article about the danger of nuclear reactors next to rising seas belonged to one of the worst online news sources. (I say this because I believe real journalism should not contain a bias, but I also like to give credit on a good news story.) The ultra liberal, conservative bashing, Huffington Post actually did a great story on the possible dangers of these East Coast reactors next to the ocean. One interesting quote read:

But most nuclear power facilities were built well before scientists understood just how high sea levels might rise in the future. And for power plants, the most serious threat is likely to come from surges during storms. Higher sea levels mean that flooding will travel farther inland, creating potential hazards in areas that may have previously been considered safe. During Superstorm Sandy, for example, flooding threatened the water *intake systems at the Oyster Creek and Salem nuclear power plants in New Jersey. As a safety precaution, both plants were powered down. But even when a plant is not operating, the spent fuel stored on-site, typically uranium, will continue to emit heat and must be cooled using equipment that relies on the plant's own power. Flooding can cause a loss of power, and in serious conditions it can damage backup generators. Without a cooling system, reactors can overheat and damage the facility to the point of releasing radioactive material.***

The article quoted gave an insightful look at flooding. It showed the foolishness of the engineers that designed these places next to the mighty Atlantic Ocean. As in mankind's nature, we tend to see dollars before we see the destruction. Is it really that wise for us to believe the East Coast of the United States will never suffer a tsunami of similar or greater power than that of the one we witnessed in Japan? Only time will truly tell.

There are numerous people predicting the East Coast tsunami. Some of them are Christians and some of them are not. In my line of work I have met numerous people that have left their coastal homes and decided to move inland to areas of higher elevation. I have seen two visions of massive flooding hitting the East Coast, but I also know that it does not necessarily mean water. Biblically speaking, floods can sometimes represent an invading army:

So shall they fear the name of the LORD from the west, and his glory from the rising of the sun. When the enemy shall come in like a flood, the Spirit of the LORD shall lift up a standard against him.
(Isaiah 59:19)

In this new age of terrorism, a conventional war is no longer fought with predictable outcomes. Nation states will give financial support to radical extremists to further the nation states financial agenda. Financing a small army to infiltrate the United States is no longer the work of fictional television shows but a stark reality. In recent years, the United States has witnessed a "wave" of undocumented immigrants with the sole purpose of executing terrorist activities on American soil. So if you ask me, the tsunami has already hit, we just have not seen the destruction yet. The tsunami of war and the tsunami of water are equally vicious. No matter which type of tsunami comes to the United States, your best preparation is to be in the "ark". I am not talking about the huge boat that protected Noah and his family. The ark I am referring to is the ark of Jesus Christ. It is this spiritual ark that will guide you and protect you in the tough times to come.

Confirmation or Coincidence?

In 1998, millions of Americans witnessed the excellent leadership of an African American President during a crisis. For the good of the country, this commander in chief instituted martial law and suspended the constitution of the United States. This president was played by Morgan Freeman and it was in the movie called ***Deep Impact***. The movie showed the viewing public the results of a meteorite landing in the Atlantic Ocean and causing a massive tsunami that destroyed the East Coast of the United States. Viewers also had the opportunity to witness the U.S. government's plan of action when such an event happens: All of the politicians and high ranking military get into the secure bunkers, meanwhile us peasants have to figure it out. Whew! Aren't we lucky that it was all make believe?

Sources

*George Washington: A biography by Washington Irving, p. 270

**http://www.huffingtonpost.com/2014/05/19/maps-rising-seas-storms-threaten-flood-coastal-nuclear-power-plants_n_5233306.html

Chapter 16

Gift of gab

Growing up in Miami, Florida for part of my life as well as Peekskill, New York, I have noticed when people display the "gift of gab". The "gift of gab" is a terminology used for a smooth talker. I define it as someone who can effectively communicate to people in all settings regardless of cultural norms and differences. These people use their gift of communication for good or evil. For example a street pimp will use the "gift of gab" to convince a young girl to sell her body to bring him (the pimp) financial gain. Of course that is evil behavior but we allow the same type of behavior from our elected officials in the Western World. Politicians use their "gift of gab" to convince people to vote for them, knowing they will abuse the powers given to them once in office. Yet, they sounded so convincing during the campaign!

Many preppers think they will use their gift of gab to escape harm's way in the future. These preppers figure that they will be able to smooth talk anyone including farmers, soldiers and psychopaths. In some cases, the person with the power of persuasion may be able to work a deal favorable for both parties involved, yet a question lingers in my mind: What if the person does not speak English (or your native tongue)?

If the situation is serious, you will have a problem on your hand that no preparedness book will tell you how to solve. Your "gift of gab" will be useless if not limited. This language barrier is a concern for many preppers. Should they learn to speak Mandarin Chinese, Russian, or even Arabic? It's a topic of discussion many preppers bring up. Here are the possible scenarios being discussed:

- Suppose the United States is invaded by Russia, North Korea and Venezuela? Should I speak the language of the invaders to gain influence or blend in?

- Suppose radical Islamists take over England? If I learned to speak fluent Arabic, wouldn't it help me avoid persecution?

- Suppose the United States suffered a devastating natural disaster and the government relocated us to Mexico? Would it not make sense to be able to speak fluent Spanish?

- Suppose the United States economy collapsed and the Chinese bailed us out? Should I learn to speak Mandarin Chinese to be able to broker deals with the Chinese real estate brokers as they come to seize bank owned properties?

These scenarios may sound far fetched to some people but in the preparedness world we understand the proverbial "changing of the guard." History has shown that when nations fell, the invaders tended to show favor to the people that could speak their home language. For example, when I speak with Iraq war veterans, they always remember the local Iraqi that knew how to speak English. This is the local guy that would come by the military base with DVDs, CDs, video games or even illicit drugs. He would provide a much needed service for the men on the base, meanwhile enriching himself and his family.

Foreign invasions are not only done by war. Another way a country can invade another is financially. It is a tactic used by many nation states throughout history. For example, one of my friends is considering entering the political scene in Jamaica. He has noticed that the current Jamaican politicians are letting the Chinese government invest billions of dollars into the island. These investments will hurt future generations because the Chinese will use their financial foothold to employ Chinese workers and not the native Jamaican workforce. Unless the Jamaican government changes its ways, a young Jamaican's best hope at financial stability is to learn the Chinese language and try to provide a service for the influx of Chinese immigrants.

Now let me get back to my point: If God has led you to learn another language, perhaps there is a reason for it. In the future, you may be one of the people chatting to the foreign soldiers when they enter U.S. soil during World War III. If you are in England in the future, perhaps you may be one of the people speaking fluent Arabic as the Islamic banking system saves London's corrupt financial center. People of all belief systems commonly say "there is a reason for everything". To the Christian, we hold the scripture that says, "The steps of a good man, are ordered by the Lord." (Psalm 37:23)

People inside the prepping world are beginning to understand why it is important to have the "gift of gab". Depending on where you are in the world during the next financial collapse, your ability to communicate to people in a crisis will be key. Now let me show you the gift of gab "Jesus style". My friend Pastor Emmanuel left his home in Rwanda to speak at a conference in Germany. Upon his arrival in Germany he was horrified to discover that his translator missed his connecting flight. The people at the conference were anxious to hear about the supernatural events that happened in his life during the Rwandan holocaust. Emmanuel prayed for God to give him a miracle in this unforeseen crisis. God instructed Emmanuel to go to the crisis because he would provide him a translator. Emmanuel stretched his faith and went to the conference. Nervously he went to the podium and began to speak. Emmanuel figured that God would provide a translator from a random person in the audience. Instead, fluent German flowed through Emmanuel's lips. By the way he spoke, Emmanuel sounded like a man educated in Germany during his two hour lecture to the German audience. An unexplainable miracle took place during Emmanuel's crisis. A similar event happened in the Bible:

₆Now when this was noised abroad, the multitude came together, and were confounded, because that every man heard them speak in his own language.
₇And they were all amazed and marveled, saying one to another, Behold, are not all these which speak Galilaeans?
₈And how hear we every man in our own tongue, wherein we were born?
(Acts 2:6-8)

This supernatural "gift of gab" is not an isolated incidence. My mentor John Parault was doing some ministry work overseas. At one particular meeting he encountered a young Japanese woman that came by the small church meeting at the request of a friend. Although she was visiting friends in England, she barely spoke the English language. Pastor John decided to tell her how much Jesus loves her. Everyone reminded John that the girl could not speak English but that didn't faze John. He took her hand and began to pray and said, "Lord, please let this young lady know how much you love her." At that moment, fluent Japanese words came out of John's mouth. Everyone in the room stood in shock because they knew John has never been to Japan and he was from the backwoods of Louisiana by way of the southern United States. After he finished speaking, the young woman jumped and down with tears of joy saying "Jesus loves me, Jesus loves me!"

And these signs shall follow them that believe; In my name shall they cast out devils; they shall speak with new tongues;
(Mark 16:17)

The scene that happened with my friend John is the result of someone using the gift of gab "Jesus style". Suppose you are in a survival situation and you do not speak the language needed at the moment? My answer to this is to ask God to give you the gift of tongues. The gift of tongues is available to any Christian filled with the Holy Spirit, regardless of your denomination. However, I must point out it is a gift that God gives out, the same way he gives some Christians the gifts of healing and prophecy. From my observation and experience, this gift will come when you simply ask God to give it to you. God gives it to some people immediately, meanwhile He lets others wait years for the gift; like in my case. Some people get the gift of foreign earthly languages, while others receive a heavenly language which fellow humans cannot understand unless God allows it. The Bible clearly says:

4Now there are diversities of gifts, but the same Spirit.
5And there are differences of administrations, but the same Lord.
6And there are diversities of operations, but it is the same God which worketh all in all.
7But the manifestation of the Spirit is given to every man to profit withal.
8For to one is given by the Spirit the word of wisdom; to another the word of knowledge by the same Spirit;
9To another faith by the same Spirit; to another the gifts of healing by the same Spirit;
10To another the working of miracles; to another prophecy; to another discerning of spirits; to another divers kinds of tongues; to another the interpretation of tongues:
11But all these worketh that one and the selfsame Spirit, dividing to every man severally as he will.
(1 Corinthians 12:4-11)

Street Credentials

Before some of you turn the pages because this section of the book offends you, I plead with you to hear my story on this matter. God actually used street credentials to prove to me that the gift of tongues were real because I used to think people that spoke in tongues were:

A) Making pretend / Faking the experience
B) Hyper Religious
C) Crazy or Drunk

Here is how God dealt with me on the matter. My late brother Wayne had converted to following Jesus Christ in the early 90s. All the guys in the hood respected Wayne's street credentials because he was a lady's man. He had the ability to date any girl he wanted and guys in the old neighborhood respected that. So it really was a shock in the neighborhood when everyone found out he became a born again Christian. Since he was the type of dude that didn't fake anything, it surprised me one afternoon to overhear him praying in fluent Hebrew in his bedroom. I knew it was Hebrew because one of my best childhood friends was Jewish and I have sat in on many of his family functions. My mom was also a maid for some Jews on Miami Beach, and since I accompanied my mom to work, I would hear many Jewish conversations. So, as I overheard my older brother, a Jamaican immigrant living in crime infested North Miami all of a sudden speak fluent Hebrew in his prayers, I began to see that maybe this "tongues" thing is for real. Here was a black dude that used to recite the comedian Eddie Murphy's best four letter cuss words now speaking to God in a language that I know he never learned in school!?!? The proof for me was right there.

Tongues for Preppers

There are many preppers that are convinced that the United States will suffer an invasion from foreign forces. As a Christian, I do not have any desire to kill another human being, especially if that person is also a Christian. We must realize that both the Chinese and Russian military have a large number of Christians within their ranks. Those young men will follow orders just like our young men followed orders into Afghanistan and Iraq. If the opportunity arises for me to speak with these men to reduce the bloodshed between our countries during the next World War, I will ask God to hone my tongue to their language. I know God will bless me with this request as well as any other believer that has the faith to do it when the time comes, because the Bible clearly says:

Blessed are the peacemakers: for they shall be called the children of God.
(Matthew 5:9)

The reason why I have decided to inform the preparedness community about the gift of tongues is threefold:

1) This gift can be used to communicate with people of another culture when the need arises.

2) This gift can be used as a weapon of warfare in the spiritual and physical realm.

3) This gift can serve as "secret telephone line" to God. It enables the very essence of your soul to have a private conversation with the creator.

Speaking Warfare

I know of many female preppers that are single or perhaps widowed. Some of you may be reading this book. Nothing is by accident and I hope you really digest the next paragraph. The gift of tongues is a weapon with better results than a can of mace. Many Christians believe it can disarm a demon or summon an Angel to your aid. Since people of all cultures recognize a demonic influence over hardcore criminals, perhaps the next story may give you single ladies some hope.

A friend of mine named Linda from Virginia was returning to her car late one night at her local Kmart. As she sat in the car and gathered her things together, she noticed a hooded man in her rear view mirror. The man was staring at her menacingly all the while glancing over his shoulders for witnesses before attacking. Linda was alarmed since her windows were already down, and the parking lot was nearly empty. Horrified because of the rampant crime in her area, she immediately closed her eyes and prayed aloud in tongues. Instantly, Linda heard a loud shriek. She opened her eyes and saw the would be criminal running for his life through the parking lot. Linda looked around bewildered because she was the only person outside that night. She built up the courage to go back in the store and ask for the security guard. The security guard told her she was lucky because there was a serial rapist in the area and he snatched two of his victims from the same parking lot!

Warfare in Government

As a writer, I learned that you have to sometimes protect your sources for fear of retribution. So I will not mention the exact nature of this meeting nor the government agencies involved.

One day I had an important meeting with a government official. I needed an important document from this official, so needless to say I was aggravated upon my arrival to hear that the official I came to see was in a car accident. The rest of the staff seemed too busy to care that I drove 3 hours and they refused to help me with the documents. I walked out of the office and began praying in tongues for a breakthrough. All of sudden, a lady from the office walked out and kindly advised me to check the government office building next door. It seemed impossible because the government office next door was high security and under a totally different jurisdiction. I prayed in tongues some more and walked to the next high security building without any invitation. Miraculously, the high security government office treated me like a foreign dignitary and walked me personally to their supervisor. The supervisor put all of his important work aside, then used all of his credentials to assist me in getting me the documents I needed within the hour! (If anyone reading this understands the scrutiny involved with high security federal government buildings then they will understand the miracle that happened!)

If you're a prepper and you get the gift of tongues, use it to get yourself into places that you normally cannot get into!

Warfare over Addictions

During one of my trips to England, I volunteered some time at Rotherham Pentecostal Church to help with their weekly feed the hungry program. As people come inside for a hot meal, the staff always has to keep an eye out for troublemakers. One particular day a man high on drugs sat at a dinner table. Due to the tracks on his arm, we could logically assume the main drug in his system was heroine. He was so high, he was pretending he was eating food with a real fork and sharp knife. When people tried to speak with him he would not even notice. He became a danger to the people near him and himself because he would occasionally swing the knife and fork in erratic fashion. Some of the people eating were beginning to leave in fear of an explosive situation. Instead of calling the police, the Pastor and I put one of our hands each on the utensils in his hand. Then we placed our other hands on the man's shoulders and began to pray over him. The Pastor of the church began to pray in tongues over the man meanwhile I prayed in normal English. In about two minutes, the darkness in the man's eyes brightened and he became sober. He looked at us both and said, "Thank you, thank you."

This is an example of using the gift of tongues in physical and spiritual warfare. The physical effects of the narcotic in the man's nervous system and blood were immediately neutralized. On the spiritual side, the demonic presence upon the man was lifted off the man. So much so that he accepted Jesus Christ as his Savior on the very spot!

Secret Communication

During a war, it is not uncommon for the military to use private communication between units. The private communication is usually a code that is immensely difficult to be broken for the sake of secrecy. In World War II, the allies used the unwritten language of the Navajo Indians to pass secret messages. The best code breakers of the Japanese military or the German army could not decode the secret communications of the Navajo Indians fighting for the United States military, thus tilting the outcome of World War II. These heroic men earned the name of "Windtalkers" and a Hollywood movie was made about them.

The supernatural world works the same way in many regards. The devil and his minions are constantly trying to figure out God's next big plan. Since God's next big plan on earth usually involves human beings, its their job to thwart those plans. The gift of tongues provides a secret communication line to the Creator of the Universe. When we are in trouble and we pray in our normal everyday language, demonic entities sometimes sneak around to eavesdrop on your request. For those of you that are well versed with the Bible, but have a hard time believing my last statement, let's take a close look at the book of Daniel chapter 10 shall we? As the prophet Daniel was praying and fasting for answers, an Angel was sent by God to answer them. However before the Angel showed up to give him answers, a demonic entity named the prince of Persia tried to stop the Angel from answering Daniel's prayer:

12Then said he unto me, Fear not, Daniel: for from the first day that thou didst set thine heart to understand, and to chasten thyself before thy God, thy words were heard, and I am come for thy words. 13But the prince of the kingdom of Persia withstood me one and twenty days: but, lo, Michael, one of the chief princes, came to help me; and I remained there with the kings of Persia.
14Now I am come to make thee understand what shall befall thy people in the latter days: for yet the vision is for many days.
(Daniel 10:12-14)

The prince of Persia was not an earthly man because an earthly man does not have the ability to do all these things simultaneously: listen in on a man's prayer, gain knowledge that the man is fasting from food, and then fight with the archangel Michael for twenty-one days. The prophet Daniel's prayer was heard not only by God's heavenly army, but by the demonic forces as well. If Daniel was using a secret code in his prayer like the Navajo did during World War II, his prayers could have been answered faster. That is exactly what the gift of tongues can do in a spiritual war!

Please understand this: if you are a believer in the God of Abraham, Isaac and Jacob: You are at war! Ever since you came out of your mother's womb the devil has been plotting on killing you and your loved ones. In any war, communication is the key between opposing factions. It does not matter if the combatants are angels, demons, Taliban, Navy Seals, or zombies. The people in the war must always have a discreet communication line without access to enemy ears. In the spiritual war that has been raging since mankind arrived on the planet, the devil has always tried to keep his ear close to the battlefield. The apostle Paul wrote about spiritual warfare and speaking in tongues at numerous times in the Bible. However, to prove my point about speaking to God in total privacy, I will point out a verse the apostle Paul wrote from two different translations of the Bible:

<u>King James Bible</u>
For he that speaketh in an unknown tongue speaketh not unto men, but unto God: for no man understandeth him; howbeit in the spirit he speaketh mysteries.

<u>New Living Translation</u>
For if you have the ability to speak in tongues, you will be talking only to God, since people won't be able to understand you. You will be speaking by the power of the Spirit, but it will all be mysterious.

(1 Corinthians 14:2)

Conclusion

The stories I mentioned are some of the examples of the things that the gift of tongues can do. Do not feel like you are not a Christian if do not have this gift. As I mentioned earlier, God didn't give me the gift for years. My mentor, the late John Parault, was a southern Baptist Pastor for over twenty years before receiving the gift of tongues! (A miracle in itself, because most Baptists think the gifts were just for the disciples of Jesus time.) It is just a gift that every prepper that proclaims to be a Christian can obtain by faith and then use it when the tough times come. If you never speak in tongues, just be sure that you love people like Jesus did. By studying the apostle Paul, he mentions that it is better to have the gift of love (charity), rather than speaking in tongues. (I Corinthians 13)

Again, the purpose of this book is to show my fellow preppers that it will be their spiritual preparation to carry them through the tough times ahead!

Authors Note: Many people have reported receiving the gift after simply asking God for it in prayer, meanwhile others have received the gift after a pastor laid hands on them while praying. If you seek more information regarding the gift of tongues, I highly suggest you go to the best source: God. After praying to God for clarification on this gift, read and study the following chapters in your Bible:

Acts 2 (read all)
Acts 19:6
Romans 8:26
1 Corinthians 13 (read all)
1 Corinthians 14 (read all)
Mark 16:17
Isaiah 28:11

Chapter 17

Blind Justice Or Justice for the Blind?

In this chapter we will discuss blindness, but not the way you think. When a person hears the word blindness, they normally think of a person with a disability which hinders their optical vision. While this chapter may touch on that version of blindness, I would like to speak about the dangers of spiritual blindness, as well as the application of blindness in warfare. Once preppers understand the full ramification of this word, this dialogue may enhance their relationship with God as well as their prepping endeavors.

Let me state that I do not take physical blindness lightly. People are born blind and some people lose their sight during their lifetime due to accidents, disease, or aging. I believe that God has a plan for every human being on this planet, including the person with a physical disability. However, when someone is spiritually blind, therein lays the true handicap. A spiritually blind person has difficulties with discerning fact from fiction and truth from lies. They believe lies like "God will take care of me" or "the government will take care of it". It is difficult for them to get revelations on the simple logic of prepping because of their apathy.

God could have had Angels build the ark for Noah or supernaturally flown Noah to heaven and then returned him to earth after the flood. God could have let grain supernaturally rain from heaven down on Joseph during the famine in Egypt. God could have let Peter and Paul supernaturally multiply food during the famine they experienced in the year A.D. 46, but for some reason, God chose for his people to make preparations during these experiences. Their spiritual eyes were opened to the changes God was making in their environment.

Many of the preppers reading this book have a great set of spiritual eyes, yet we all have friends or family members that do not. During my tenure as a survival food consultant, I have encountered many people that face scrutiny from their spouse for prepping. The amount of people I have encountered that has a spouse that ridicules them for emergency preparedness is alarming. I commonly hear things like:

"Brother Keith, my wife thinks I am crazy for buying long term foods and bottled water."

"My husband does not want to hear anything about doom and gloom."

"My wife would rather spend the money on a vacation."

"My husband keeps saying the government will take care of it."

"My wife will not listen to any of it because she believes that God will rapture us to heaven before anything bad happens."

As you can see from the comments listed, these type of comments are quite the norm. The scenarios of different people mentioned above generally suffer from a spirit of blindness. This spirit tends to keep people in their comfort zone. If you have loved ones that suffer terribly from this spirit, let me give you the solution. Find another person that believes in God just like you do and join with them in agreement to pray over that loved one that does not want to begin prepping. This may sound corny but I have done it with many people and the results were phenomenal. The reason why it works is because of the words of Jesus:

Again I say unto you, That if two of you shall agree on earth as touching any thing that they shall ask, it shall be done for them of my Father which is in heaven.
(Matthew 18:19)

It really is that simple. In some cases it's almost hilarious when the spouse begins to see the results! The amount of people that tell me later, "Brother, my husband has really come around now!" or "My wife is now buying extra canned goods and bottled water!" is amazing.

Here is an example of the prayer you should say with another person concerning the relative or loved one that refuses to prepare:

Heavenly Father; we lift up our friend (name here)
(name here) is refusing to see the reality of the day we are living in
(name here) does not see the wisdom in making preparations
(name here) does not want to hear anything about the subject
We are asking you Father to rip the scales off his/her eyes
We are asking you Father to clean the wax out of his/her ears
We are asking you to give (name here) a spirit of wisdom and not fear
We are asking you to give (name here) a spirit of courage to take action
In Jesus name we pray, Amen!

Email me with the results. I always love to hear them!

Blindness in Warfare

Preppers need to understand the usage of blindness as a weapon in warfare. We see images of Guantanamo Bay detainees, Viet Nam prisoners of war, and even radical Islamists groups in movies or the nightly news all the time. Do we ever notice the modus operandi of all these groups? They all find it absolutely necessary to place a blindfold upon the eyes of their enemy. In some cases they will physically damage the eyesight of an enemy. Since God created war and peace, could blindness actually be a tool of warfare by both God and man? My question was answered in the Bible:

8Then the king of Syria warred against Israel, and took counsel with his servants, saying, In such and such a place shall be my camp.
9And the man of God sent unto the king of Israel, saying, Beware that thou pass not such a place; for thither the Syrians are come down.
10And the king of Israel sent to the place which the man of God told him and warned him of, and saved himself there, not once nor twice.
11Therefore the heart of the king of Syria was sore troubled for this thing; and he called his servants, and said unto them, Will ye not shew me which of us is for the king of Israel?
12And one of his servants said, None, my lord, O king: but Elisha, the prophet that is in Israel, telleth the king of Israel the words that thou speakest in thy bedchamber.
13And he said, Go and spy where he is, that I may send and fetch him. And it was told him, saying, Behold, he is in Dothan.
14Therefore sent he thither horses, and chariots, and a great host: and they came by night, and compassed the city about.
15And when the servant of the man of God was risen early, and gone forth, behold, an host compassed the city both with horses and chariots. And his servant said unto him, Alas, my master! how shall we do?
16And he answered, Fear not: for they that be with us are more than they that be with them.
17And Elisha prayed, and said, LORD, I pray thee, open his eyes, that he may see. And the LORD opened the eyes of the young man; and he saw: and, behold, the mountain was full of horses and chariots of fire round about Elisha.
18And when they came down to him, Elisha prayed unto the LORD, and said, Smite this people, I pray thee, with blindness. And he smote them with blindness according to the word of Elisha.
(2 Kings 6:8-18)

Okay preppers, you just read the story of Elisha and his servant getting surrounded by the Syrian army. The Syrian army was not attempting to drop off Christmas cookies, in fact they were coming to kill Elisha and the servants of God. Can God still blind your enemies when things hit the fan? The answer is yes!

Let me give you an example of using blindness in warfare. In her bestselling book, **Left to Tell*****, author Immaculee Ilibagiza gives her dreadful account of living in the African nation of Rawanda during the 1994 war and genocide in her country that killed 1,000,000 people. At a critical point she was hiding in a tiny bathroom with seven other women to avoid men that were going to homes and systematically killing people from her tribe. As the men approached the home, the women engaged in a fierce prayer to God to blind the men so they could not be found. The men forcefully entered the house and searched the entire house from top to bottom with their guns and machetes drawn. However, every time they entered the bedroom that had the adjoining bathroom door, the men were made supernaturally blind to the door leading to the bathroom!

Another powerful story that comes to mind is from Viet Nam veteran Andy Wommack. While serving as an assistant to the chaplain during the war, Andy encountered a situation that should of ended in bloodshed but because he had a deep relationship with God, the warfare remained spiritual. In the novel called **Psalm 91: God's Shield of Protection**, Andy recounted an event when he and an Army Chaplain left the base in a jeep to visit a Vietnamese pastor in enemy territory. Andy Wommack recalls:

"After visiting the pastor for about thirty minutes or so, the chaplain asked him, 'Is there any Viet Cong activity here?" The pastor assured him there was a great deal of Viet Cong activity. He had us look out the window to a long building directly across the street, which he said was a Viet Cong headquarters.

Needless to say there were Viet Cong walking around with AK-47s, the Russian-made weapon. They were not American friendly and they were right across the street, with our jeep in plain sight. The chaplain got so scared that all he wanted was to get out of there as quickly as possible. There we were – two Americans in uniform, in an Army jeep, driving through these Vietnamese guards who had Ak-47s on their shoulders. We know they saw us because, as we drove through they would get out of the way of the jeep to let us pass. They didn't say a thing to us and never pointed a weapon at us as we drove through the midst of them. There were about six of them, and they simply parted as we drove by.

The whole thing was so incomprehensible that the chaplain and I just looked at each other, speechless. I'm not sure what happened. There is no telling what God did to enable us to get out of there alive. There is no natural explanation for those Viet Cong not to have taken us captive or killed us on the spot..."
(Psalm 91: God's Shield of Protection p. 187-88)

Now those two examples previously mentioned are God blinding and confusing an enemy. Make no mistake about it, those people were in real life survival situations. There are times when God will allow it to be done person to person without the use of a physical weapon. The Apostle Paul proved this during his ministry:

5And when they were at Salamis, they preached the word of God in the synagogues of the Jews: and they had also John to their minister.
6And when they had gone through the isle unto Paphos, they found a certain sorcerer, a false prophet, a Jew, whose name was Barjesus:
7Which was with the deputy of the country, Sergius Paulus, a prudent man; who called for Barnabas and Saul, and desired to hear the word of God.
8But Elymas the sorcerer (for so is his name by interpretation) withstood them, seeking to turn away the deputy from the faith.

9Then Saul, (who also is called Paul,) filled with the Holy Ghost, set his eyes on him,
10And said, O full of all subtilty and all mischief, thou child of the devil, thou enemy of all righteousness, wilt thou not cease to pervert the right ways of the Lord?
11And now, behold, the hand of the Lord is upon thee, and thou shalt be blind, not seeing the sun for a season. And immediately there fell on him a mist and a darkness; and he went about seeking some to lead him by the hand.
12Then the deputy, when he saw what was done, believed, being astonished at the doctrine of the Lord.
(Acts 13:5-12)

If the prophet Elisha performed this miracle on an army of men, and the Apostle Paul did the same miracle to a sorcerer, would a prepper filled with the Holy Spirit be able to do the same if the situation required it? I believe it is absolutely possible because I have personal friends that proved it.

(Author's Note: This level of warfare is for mature Christians only. Do not attempt unless you receive a direct word from God.)

In my chapter titled "Physical Fitness or Spiritual Fitness", I mentioned my friend Pastor Emmanuel. He is the gentleman that survived in Rwanda for two weeks with his intestines hanging out and God supernaturally healing him. One day a medical doctor tried to publicly humiliate Emmanuel for his story. The doctor called Emmanuel a liar and denounced the existence of God. Just like the Apostle Paul, Emmanuel became filled with a righteous indignation. Instead of punching the doctor in the nose, Emmanuel said, "In the name of Jesus, I command blindness on you for 3 days!" Immediately, the doctor lost his eyesight and began screaming for help. The end result came three days later when the doctor ditched his atheist beliefs and received Jesus Christ as his Lord. The doctor's eyesight came back and he now works in ministry!

Behold, I give unto you power to tread on serpents and scorpions, and over all the power of the enemy: and nothing shall by any means hurt you.
Luke 10:19

America's Spiritual Blindness

To any prepper with a spiritual set of eyes, I would like you read this passage from the book of Genesis:

1And there came two angels to Sodom at even; and Lot sat in the gate of Sodom: and Lot seeing them rose up to meet them; and he bowed himself with his face toward the ground;
2And he said, Behold now, my lords, turn in, I pray you, into your servant's house, and tarry all night, and wash your feet, and ye shall rise up early, and go on your ways. And they said, Nay; but we will abide in the street all night.
3And he pressed upon them greatly; and they turned in unto him, and entered into his house; and he made them a feast, and did bake unleavened bread, and they did eat.
4But before they lay down, the men of the city, even the men of Sodom, compassed the house round, both old and young, all the people from every quarter:
5And they called unto Lot, and said unto him, Where are the men which came in to thee this night? bring them out unto us, that we may know them.
6And Lot went out at the door unto them, and shut the door after him,
7And said, I pray you, brethren, do not so wickedly.
8Behold now, I have two daughters which have not known man; let me, I pray you, bring them out unto you, and do ye to them as is good in your eyes: only unto these men do nothing; for therefore came they under the shadow of my roof.
9And they said, Stand back. And they said again, This one fellow came in to sojourn, and he will needs be a judge: now will

we deal worse with thee, than with them. And they pressed sore upon the man, even Lot, and came near to break the door.
10But the men put forth their hand, and pulled Lot into the house to them, and shut to the door.
11And they smote the men that were at the door of the house with blindness, both small and great: so that they wearied themselves to find the door.
(Genesis 19:1-11)

There is level of spiritual blindness that only God Himself deals with. It is beyond the human understanding because its evil roots are highly demonic. The root cause of spiritual blindness is sin. Uh-oh, the author said the dreaded "s" word! In America, the word sin is becoming taboo because everything is allowed. When sin reaches a peak in a culture, spiritual blindness is the by product. Powerful empires of the past such as Ancient Rome became spiritually blind to laws of our Creator. The end result of such powerful empires has always been tragic. As we watch the news reports of women getting tragically gang raped in India, people in the United States will look at the Indian culture as a whole and make a negative judgment. Americans will sometimes say, "Why doesn't the Indian government do something?" My answer to the American people is, "Have you looked in your backyard lately?"

41And why beholdest thou the mote that is in thy brother's eye, but perceivest not the beam that is in thine own eye?
42Either how canst thou say to thy brother, Brother, let me pull out the mote that is in thine eye, when thou thyself beholdest not the beam that is in thine own eye? Thou hypocrite, cast out first the beam out of thine own eye, and then shalt thou see clearly to pull out the mote that is in thy brother's eye.
(Luke 6:41-42)

The number of rapes taking place at the colleges throughout America is alarming, yet the universities attempt to downplay the issue because of financial agendas*. The same behavior is happening as we speak within the United States Military. Young military recruits are becoming the victims of brutal rapes by older officers**. This use to be a terrible issue for the female recruits but now the epidemic is affecting the male recruits at a much higher rate!

The sin of rape is a product of spiritual blindness. The United States Federal government is beginning a systematic raping of the laws which separate church and state. The New Health care law attempted to force the churches in America to fund abortion related treatments while the IRS has punished conservative Christian programs and speakers. To top it off, the Federal Government is now attempting to force the church to marry same sex couples!

Preppers in the United States, beware of the time you are living in! There is a direct correlation between rape and facing God's judgment. Whenever a society turns a blind eye to such evils in the land, God doles out His punishments. In Genesis 19, the angels and Lot represented God's church. Lot was imperfect, the Angels were perfect, and they give us an illustration of the church in a land that is spiritually blind. Instead of asking the Angels to bless them, the spiritually blind people came by to rape them! After the Angels struck them with blindness, verse eleven tells us that they "wearied themselves to find the door." The would be rapists were so spiritually blind to a judgment from God hitting their land, they continued to try to find their victims in a blind state! Instead of begging the Angels to restore their sight and begin apologizing (repenting) for their wicked behavior, these men pushed their agenda even further. The government of Sodom and Gomorrah allowed rape to be the norm of the day. The United States government is actually allowing rape on spiritual and physical levels. This is the reason why many preppers in the United States feel the urge to prepare. Turning a blind eye to evil is what brings a judgment!

Woe unto them that call evil good, and good evil; that put darkness for light, and light for darkness; that put bitter for sweet, and sweet for bitter!
(Isaiah 5:20)

Sources

*http://nypost.com/2015/02/27/how-the-hunting-ground-uncovers-the-campus-rape-epidemic/
**http://www.gq.com/long-form/male-military-rape
*** *Left to Tell by Immaculee Ilibagiza*

Chapter 18

Voices

This is a crucial time for you to evaluate the voices in your surroundings. Is your prepping motivated by the voice of wisdom or the voice of fear? Let me give you an example of the voice of fear: I had a customer that was prepping for a comet named Elenin. It was supposed to be a small comet flying near earth that had the potential of direct impact or a close fly by. The potential disaster on earth for a comet flying by in a close proximity is mind boggling to say the least. It could trigger numerous types of natural disasters on earth within minutes and the potential loss of life would be great. However, the evidence of this comet coming near the earth was suspicious. Numerous different astronomers from around the world were debating the very existence of the comet.

Rather than making a balanced decision with the information she was getting from the internet, the customer was preparing with fear. She immediately sold some of her business interests and even asked me if she should max out her credit cards! I sensed the spirit of fear moving on this precious lady. I let her know that she should do no such thing because she does not need a financial issue if this comet does not arrive. I noticed the source of her fear in a short period of time. She listened to fear based radio programs on the internet and would visit the local psychics for spiritual guidance. The voices that constantly bombarded her mind were coming from bad sources.

Let this story rest with all preppers; do not make the mistake of this woman. Do not listen to fear based radio programs and watch fear based entertainment on your television screens if you do not have the ability to discern facts from fiction. The voices of these programs will have a profound effect on your subconscious if you can not objectively discern the information. You want your prepping endeavors to be made from wisdom, not fear. The voice behind fear does not allow rationale decision making.

Voices of Deception

At moments in history, there are groups of Christians that conduct the same immature behavior. The voices they listen to are voices of deception. My best example is of the late Christian evangelist Harold Camping.* He had billboards put up across the United States predicting Judgment Day to be May 21, 2011. Thousands of followers made preparations to be supernaturally transported to heaven by selling their homes, giving away personal possessions, amongst other things. They simply listened to the voice of a deceiver. I can make that claim because Harold Camping had made earlier predictions regarding the rapture of the church and he was wrong on every one of them! The reason why he was wrong, like other Christians of the past, is because he was not listening to the voice of the Holy Spirit. If people would actually take the time to read the words Jesus said regarding the rapture and Judgment Day they could discern the voices they are hearing:

But of that day and hour knoweth no man, no, not the angels of heaven, but my Father only.
(Matthew 24:36)

My advice to every reader out there is to seek the voice of God and not the voice of man, because man will deceive you. Even the most sincere clergy men can be unknowingly tricked by a lying spirit like the false prophets mentioned in the Bible. The best way to hear God's voice is to have a life of prayer and learning the word of God yourself. Many of the people deceived by Harold Camping and the other prediction posse did not read the Bible for themselves. They relied on the interpretations of others, which is a dangerous thing to do in any religion.

And the LORD said unto him, Wherewith? And he said, I will go forth, and I will be a lying spirit in the mouth of all his prophets. And he said, Thou shalt persuade him, and prevail also: go forth, and do so.
(1 Kings 22:22)

The Voice of Barabbas

During the trial of Jesus Christ, the crowd had shouted for the release of a revolutionary named Barabbas. Pontius Pilate and his officials did not listen to their conscious, they listened to their fear. They feared a riot so they decided to crucify the innocent Jesus of Nazareth and free the revolutionary named Barabbas. Although he was one person, Barabbas represented two voices spoken that day: The voice of political correctness and the voice of civil unrest. Due to political correctness, the Roman leadership let a known terrorist go free but crucified the Christ. Politically correct decisions like this led to the Jewish revolts of Roman rule in which hundreds of thousands of people died. The Jewish leadership at the time did not obey the voice of Jesus Christ nor His teachings. Today, in the United States, it is evident that history will repeat itself. The false voice of political correctness will prohibit the labeling of sinful behavior. People are scared to "tell it like it is", especially the men in the clergy. Sin is sin and political correctness tries to hide that fact. I discovered that many preppers with some spiritual sense agree that America can not continue its path of resisting God's spiritual laws as well as the natural laws of the constitution of the United States. The false voice of political correctness divides a country into tiny shreds of a broken cup. It will no longer stand to hold anything!

24And if a kingdom be divided against itself, that kingdom cannot stand.
25And if a house be divided against itself, that house cannot stand.
(Mark 3:24-25)

Instead of listening to the voice of Jesus Christ, some preppers are listening to the voice of criminal revolutionaries. The other voice behind the release of Barabbas is the spirit of civil unrest which leads to civil war. We have some mentally unstable preppers that think the citizenry should draw arms on the government. Perhaps three hundred years ago they may have had a valid point, but in this day and age of technology, this is suicidal thinking. We as preppers must realize that God is the one that establishes the government, and if the leaders do evil practices, God is the one who removes them. If the people of the United States can listen to the voice of Jesus Christ, a civil war could easily be avoidable. People will not shed blood over racial tensions, uneven wealth distribution, police brutality and banker bailouts. God just wants people to turn to Him with a repentant heart and then He will begin to supernaturally fix the many woes that ail our country.

If my people, which are called by my name, shall humble themselves, and pray, and seek my face, and turn from their wicked ways; then will I hear from heaven, and will forgive their sin, and will heal their land.
(1 Chronicles 7:14)

As a prepper and a preacher, I do not see the overall masses of the United States dropping to their knees in mass repentance, which is to simply tell God "We are sorry for our sins." The only way that will happen is through pain. Like an unruly child getting a spanking from his loving parent, that is how America will learn. A spanking will bring the repentance God requires to bring national healing. When people heard the warnings of Jesus concerning the destruction of Jerusalem, many of them made preparations and didn't suffer the onslaught of the Roman army. Today, in the Western World, especially the United States, now is your time to make preparations. The warnings have been given. It is up to you to decide which voice you should listen to!

Your Voice Or His Voice

In closing this book, I would like to elaborate about the voices around us. We constantly hear voices through our television, radio, and Mp3 players. These voices can entertain, teach, deceive and program our decisions in everyday life. Our children hear these voices every time they enter the school room. The voices they hear can build them up like a skyscraper or utterly destroy them like the twin towers on 9/11. The same thing applies to adults. The voices a grown man can face in this day can tell him to provide the best life for his family or to desert them the minute his girlfriend reveals she is pregnant. The voices a grown woman may hear in this day may tell her to celebrate the fact that she is pregnant or to abort the child because her career is more important. Which voice do we listen too?

My answer is simple but solid truth. We should aim to listen to the voice of God, especially my friends in the preparedness movement. History has proven that preppers are a rare breed of human being. In some cases, we are either way out in left field or we are way out in right field. The proper place to be is right in the middle, focusing your ears for divine guidance. The best way to have your ears fine tuned into what God is saying is by asking Jesus Christ into your heart and starting a life of prayer. Your prayer life will literally be the barrier that stops the angel of death in his tracks.

During his tour in Iraq, my friend David also known as the Youtube sensation "Southern Prepper" told me of the day he heard from God. During his off time, David decided to hand wash one of his sweaty shirts. It was a normal routine when he wasn't busy and he could quickly get his shirts to dry quickly in the hot Middle Eastern weather. As he finished washing his shirt and made his walk to his barrack, he heard a voice in his head say, "Go back, wash your shirt again."

Trying to ignore the voice, David kept walking to the barrack. The voice wasn't audible but it was louder in his mind. It said, "Go back and wash your shirt now!"

Listening to the voice, David turned around and walked back to the area to wash his shirt a second time. He checked to see if he missed any stains but didn't see any blemishes. Perplexed, he decided to wash the shirt again for good measure. Just then he heard the sound of rapid machine gun fire. The men nearby were ducking for cover. In about one minute the gunshots stopped. People were scrambling to see if an enemy soldier made it into their base. David heard the men from his barrack screaming. As he went to investigate with some other men, they discovered a belt fed machine gun was accidentally knocked over by a rookie private. The gun hit the floor and began firing bullets in every direction. About seven men were shot within the course of a minute. If David had ignored the voice to wash his shirt a second time, he would have been one of the victims. David is convinced that he was able to hear God's warning because he begins every day with prayer.

I love them that love me; and those that seek me early shall find me.
(Proverbs 8:17)

My friends Richard and Rhima confirmed this notion of hearing God's voice. When Rhima was single in 2006, she heard God tell her two life changing things after her prayer time. She said God told her, "I have a husband for you and start buying ammunition." The message was strange because Rhima didn't even know how to operate a gun. In less than a year she met Richard and they became man and wife. Ironically, her husband's favorite hobby is collecting guns. So when she revealed to him what the Lord told her, he supported the idea of buying ammunition. Rhima's investment in ammunition since 2006 has paid huge dividends. The price of ammunition has tripled and she now has the option of selling it or keeping it for the future. How did Rhima get the inside information about purchasing bullets long before the nationwide ammo shortages? She made time to pray, and in return, God opened her ears to hear.

Everyone has different experiences hearing from God. In some cases it's an audible voice and in other cases it's a small inner voice. The very book you are reading is proof of this. The original draft of this book was written as a drama. Imagine reading the African American version of a James Wesley Rawles preparedness novel. I decided to pray and fast for a while before releasing the original version of the book. On one particular day when I was done praying, I heard the spirit of God tell me, "Now write the book over."

At first I kinda felt insulted, because I put countless hours into writing the first version of this book, but I realize now the purpose for re-writing it. The original version of this book was going to be like any other preparedness book. God wanted people in the preparedness world to know that He is the source and the solution for all their needs. Our preparations for the future should all start by hearing His voice.

Friends, preppers, countrymen, lend me your ears. We will face some difficult decisions in the days ahead. The most difficult decision will be: Should I help this person in need or is this person coming to harm my family? It is the question that looms in the mind of most preppers. The only way for you to answer the question correctly is to hear God's voice. It will be His voice that will guide you through the difficult times. It will be His voice that will help you make the correct decisions. It will be His voice that will keep the spirit of fear away from you. It will be His voice that will provide for you. It will be His voice that will protect you.

Protection from who you may ask? Yourself.

Let's stop listening to our fears; and let's start listening to God.

My sheep hear my voice, and I know them, and they follow me:
(John 10:17)

Source

*http://www.ibtimes.com/harold-camping-silent-after-doomsday-dud-285301

Bonus Section

If you would like to have emergency supplies (food, water, and medicines), but you are not sure where to start, hopefully this section can help you. As with all emergency foods and products, keep them stored in a cool dry place. Never put them in an attic or a hot storage shed.

Survival Foods that have a minimum shelf life of 15 years

- Freeze Dried Foods (when sealed without oxygen)

- Dry Grains like white rice, oats, etc. (when sealed without oxygen)

- Legumes like pinto beans, lentil beans, etc. (when sealed without oxygen)

- Sugar, Salt, and Raw Honey

- Check out www.foodsurvivalstore.com for examples

Basic Survival foods with 5 years of shelf life

- Canned Tuna*

- Canned Meats*

- Canned Vegetables & Fruits*

*The dates on canned food can be misleading. Theoretically, as long as a can remains intact the food inside should still be edible. The useful life of canned goods can be shortened by accidental damage or poor storage conditions. If swelling, deep rust or bad dents can be seen on the can, throw the can in the garbage. Once it's been opened, your canned food should be treated like any other perishable food. I have found the steel cans to be stronger than the aluminum cans. If you prefer steel cans, place a magnet on the can before purchasing, if the can is made of steel, the magnet will stick to it. If it is made of aluminum the magnet will not stick to the can.

- Thin sliced dehydrated fruits and veggies tend to last about two years, but they will last longer when sealed without oxygen.

- Peanut Butter (depends on storage conditions)

- Coffee – Can last longer if kept in whole bean form, and sealed without oxygen.

- Tea- Can last longer if sealed without oxygen

- White Pasta and Ramen Noodles – Can last longer if sealed without oxygen

- Hard Candy- Can last longer if sealed without oxygen and can be a great morale booster!

- Powdered milk- Can last longer if sealed without oxygen

- Dried herbs and spices- Can last longer if sealed without oxygen

- Coconut Oil has a long shelf when kept in cool dark place.

Survival Food used by military, police, and emergency services

MRES are a short abbreviation for Meals Ready to Eat. It's a self-contained field ration used by militaries around the world. The contents will vary but they are commonly used where organized food facilities are not available. They can be eaten without any cooking and the shelf life can be ten years. It would be wise to drink plenty of water with them because of the salt content and lack of fiber.

Additional Advice about food storage

- Go to www.youtube.com and type in "mylar bags and oxygen absorbers" for ideas

- Never leave food in hot environments such as an attic or a sun exposed storage shed.

- Always consider a child as an adult when conducting food storage calculations because their appetites increase with growth.

- Any extra food stored can be used to help feed a friend or neighbor.

- If you purchase an emergency food bucket with single serving packs, please be advised that the caloric intake and measured serving size is usually small. Eat a recommended serving size for dinner to see if your stomach is satisfied.

- When in doubt, buy extra white rice. It can feed a lot of people at an affordable price and it has a long shelf life.

- To keep weevils and bugs out of your grains, try sprinkling Food Grade Diatomaceous Earth powder before storing away your grains. It's an organic method of pest control used by grain farmers around the world.

- Brown Rice may not last as long due to a slightly small oil content. My experience with brown rice has shown me that **it must** be stored without oxygen and kept in a cool, dark area.

Water

In everyday life, unforeseen emergency or disaster, you will always need water. It is needed for cooking, cleaning and drinking. Here are some suggestions:

- Always keep extra bottled water available.

- Buy a water filter that can filter out viruses and bacteria. I will not push one particular brand over the other, but I recommend having a water filter that is strong enough to remove Escherichia coli or the more popular name E. coli. This bacteria is normally the most prevalent in situations when clean water is unavailable. Most chain store brand water filters are not strong enough to remove E. coli from the water. I suggest using the internet to find the water filter that fits your needs or specialty stores for campers and hikers. Check www.foodsurvivalstore.com for water filters!

- Get a small water filtration bottle for traveling. If you had to walk ten miles, these are handy if you need to take water from a stream or pond.

- Get a non-electric filtration system for your home. Something big enough to clean water for you and your loved ones if you needed to go outside to get water from a storm drain, pond, or stream.

- If you have the room, get a rain barrel to catch rain water should the need arise.

- Get water purification drops and tablets.

- If a hurricane/tornado is approaching, fill the bathtub with water to have emergency water available.

- Go to www.youtube.com and type "water storage" for ideas and suggestions

Basic First Aid and Overall Health

- Aspirin / Acetaminophen

- Ibuprofen

- Antibiotics including colloidal silver

- Antacids

- Antihistamines

- Pepto-Bismol or equivalent

- Cough and Mucus medicine

- Laxatives

- Sleep Aides

- Saline Spray

- Vitamins

- Extra supply of Prescription Drugs

- Bandages, Gauze, Wound Cream

- Maxi Pads, Tampons, etc.

- Soaps, Antibacterial Wipes, etc.

Preparing on a Budget

- Use coupons. Some grocery stores will double the value of your coupon on certain days. Combine that with a buy one get one free deal and you can really save. Join a coupon sharing club on Facebook or another social media site.

- Use store points shopping rewards. Store points are used in numerous ways at certain stores. They really save money when combined with coupons. Check for clearance items and you can literally walk out of the store with free stuff!

- If you have a big family, always compare bulk food prices with regular store prices.

- Go to close out stores for certain canned goods. Ask the manager if he will give you a special discount if you purchase by the case.

- If your finances are at a near poverty level (I been there), put your pride to the side and go to your local food bank. They get tons of donated food that is thrown away if people don't take them. The amount of canned foods they give away is mind boggling.

Cut out wasteful habits.

- If you smoke a pack of cigarettes a day, but you feel the need to prepare your family, perhaps you should start weaning yourself on the cigarettes. The money you use for the cigarettes over a year could probably buy your family a nice supply of emergency food.

- Cable television. Why not cut off the subscription and read more books and watch DVDs? If you have the internet, you can watch plenty of programs online for free. The $100 you spend every month for cable can buy your family a water filter and at least six months of emergency food.

- Cell phone service. Do all of your kids need fancy cell phones? Probably not. The $300 a month bill on the fancy iphones for your household will not feed you in crisis. Get a prepaid no-contract smart phone for $50 a month to cut costs. Your kids will thank you later when they are eating a good meal. Your wife will thank you when you take her to dinner with the extra money saved.

- Stop buying the $10 lunch every day. Bring a sandwich or leftovers with you for lunch. The $200 you save every month can be used to buy the bullets you were going to use to keep your family from being robbed when the police don't show up in time.

- Stop buying name brand groceries. For example, a supermarket store like Aldi specializes in generic name brand foods and products with big time savings. The money you save by buying a generic brand can add up quickly.

- Sell the assets you do not need to feed your family. For example: I have a friend that has eight classic guitars worth a significant amount of money. I suggested he sell one or two of the guitars to purchase his emergency products for his family because in a crisis those high dollar guitars will not feed them.

Real Food Storage Experiences

2 Week old Unrefrigerated Raw Meat for dinner?
A friend of mine in England discovered that vacuum packed raw meat can resist spoilage when unrefrigerated as opposed to regular raw meat wrapped in paper or shrink wrap. During a major storm in England, he lost electricity for about 10 days. Assuming the food in his outdoor garage freezer was a loss, he took out the defrosted meat packs and left them on the countertop in his garage. Two weeks passed by and he remembered the food he forgot to throw away. Horrified that he forgot to throw away the meat packs, he assumed the garage would be a smelly mess. To his surprise, everything smelled normal and the vacuum packed meats were not leaking fluid. Curious, he cut one open to smell the contents and to his surprise the meat was fine. He and his wife cooked the vacuum sealed meats in the following week and experienced no symptoms of sickness! He said his garage was an average temperature of 60 degrees Fahrenheit during the weeks the meat was left on the countertop in the garage. We could only theorize that the vacuum sealed meat packs avoided spoilage because they were devoid of oxygen and the garage was dark and cool.

15 year old Frosted Flakes for breakfast?
On a sweeter note, it has been said among preppers that cereal is not ideal for long term storage. This has been said because the grains are processed, and because of the fat content. Through experience, I have proven this theory to be partially false. I believe

it depends on the type of cereal and the storage methods. I recently helped a customer take inventory of her deceased husband's survival food supply. He had Frosted Flakes brand cereal stored in mylar bags with an oxygen absorber. Since they were stored from 1997, I was curious to know if they were spoiled. I opened a bag and put a few flakes in my mouth. My eyes widened and I yelled like Tony the Tiger, "They tasted great!"

I theorize that Frosted Flakes were still edible because they were sealed with no oxygen in a mylar bag, and the sugar coating helped in the preservation process. The dark basement they were stored in never rose past 60 degrees Fahrenheit, so the cool temperature was also a factor. To further prove they were fine, I ended up eating the whole 16 ounce bag of cereal. Yummy!

Moldy Pancake Mix
The subject of pancake mix for long term food storage is a divisive subject among the preparedness community, but I can only speak from experience. A prepper I knew in West Virginia decided to rotate his food supply. From the information he gave a mutual friend, he pulled a sealed container of pancake mix from his survival supply and cooked some pancakes. Within the next two hours he was rushed to the emergency room. After medical examination the doctor determined he was poisoned by eating mold. Evidently, it was because of eating the old pancake mix. Perhaps the seal on the pancake mix was exposed to air, but there are numerous cases I found online regarding people getting sick from old pancake mix. For preppers, it is a simple luxury food because of the "just add water" features but I feel the risks do not outweigh the benefits. Hence the reason why I avoid it for long term food storage.

Old Brown Rice
Most preppers are brainwashed to believe that brown rice is impossible to keep for long term food storage due to the oil content in the rice. People say that brown rice will not last longer than six months under normal conditions. That is not completely accurate. Brown rice can last for a few years if kept sealed without oxygen or

sprinkled with food grade diatomaceous earth. If you do either of the two methods plus keep it from sunlight, and store it in a cool, dark place, you should be able to keep the rice for a few years. I have done it personally as well as a few friends and the rice tasted just fine.

Organic Maple Syrup and Raw Honey
Most preppers assume that organic maple syrup shares the same long shelf life as raw honey. Wrong! The other day I poured some 2 year old organic maple syrup onto my kid's pancakes and out comes a big green patch of mold. I was happy I saw it and I threw away their breakfast and the half gallon container of syrup. Upon some research, I found out that organic maple syrup can develop mold over time especially when the bottle has been opened. However, in a survival situation you can remove the mold by skimming the top and boil the syrup to make it edible again.
Raw honey on the other hand does not develop mold and stays edible for years. I recently enjoyed tea at my friend Panthea's house and we enjoyed honey she saved from her beekeeping days. To my shock the honey was from 1986!

Weapons

If you read the entire book, you should know that I believe that the actual practice of the word of God is your ultimate weapon. These words are found in the 1611 version King James Bible. The supernatural events recorded in this book all had a seed from the events recorded in the Bible.

As for weapons in the natural realm, I suggest you observe your local laws of the country you live in. If the country you live in has strict gun laws, I suggest you study the legal loopholes around the laws placed as well as studying alternative weapons. Since the availability of diverse weapons in the United States are on such a massive scale, I decided to give this example for my friends in Canada and England: Lets suppose there was anarchy in the streets and the police were not responding to any calls. If a burglar with a gun was at your front door attempting to break into your flat, what could you use to stop him?

      A) prayer

      B) Bleach

      C) Wasp / Hornet Spray

      D) Cricket bat / Baseball bat

      E) Cooking Oil

      F) All the above could be used

The correct answer is the letter (F) because everything can be used to defend yourself. Obviously prayer is first because God can open the doors for numerous ways to protect you supernaturally. Bleach could be put in a bucket and then dumped on the burglar's head. The fumes will annoy him and the burning of his eyes will leave him incapacitated. The wasp/hornet spray cans shoot liquid at a distance of 20 feet. The stream of liquid has the same effect as a can of mace. The burglar will be in severe pain once it's in his face. He will lose the desire to rob anyone that day! The cricket bat can be applied numerous ways. I prefer to use it in conjunction with the cooking oil. If you don't have carpet behind the front door, quickly pour out the cooking oil a few feet behind the threshold of the front door. When a looter forces their way into a home, balance is the last thing on their mind. The momentum and lack of balance will equal a guaranteed slip and fall in the striking range of your bat. A burglar lying on the floor with a gun will have trouble lifting his weapon with the force of a bat landing on their skull!

Thank you for reading my first book: **The Prepper and the Preacher**

Sincerely,
Brother Keith

For speaking engagements email addaiinvestments@gmail.com
https://www.facebook.com/keith.iton